THE ALBUM
IS PUBLISHED
AS ORDER
OF THE MOSCOW'S
KNIGA SOCIETY

EDITORS:
B. KARPOV
I. ULYANOVA

RUSSIAN

IKPA
Soviet-Finnish
Joint Venture
MOSCOW, 1990

**PHOTOGRAPHER
A.SENTSOV**

**DESIGNERS:
V.OSIPYAN
V.POPKOV**

ORTHODOX CHURCH

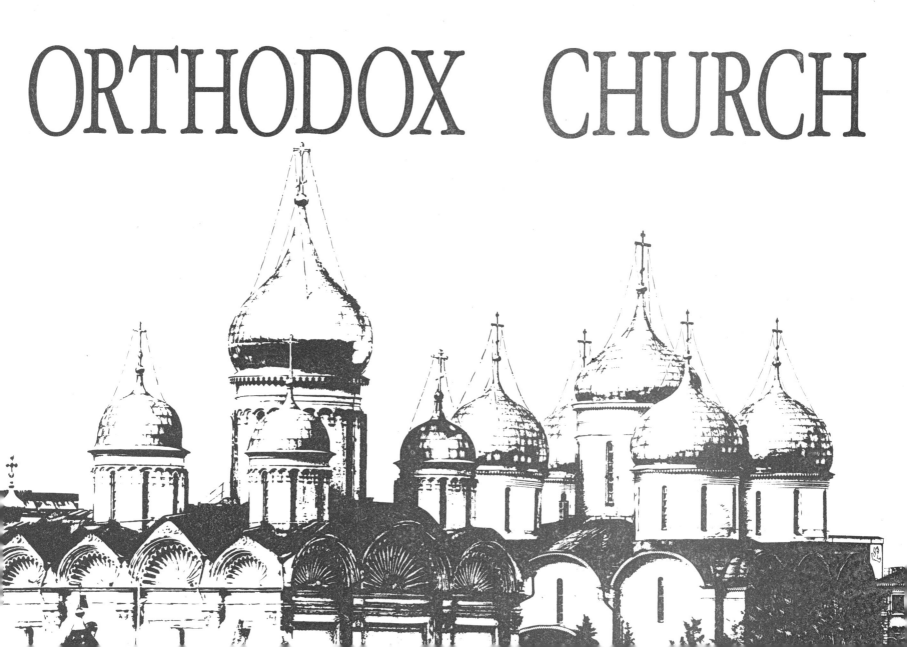

Soviet-Finnish Joint Venture **IKPA**

10, Kalashny pereulok, Moscow, 103009

ISBN 5-85202-047-8

$$P\frac{0403000000\text{-}17}{939\text{-}90}$$

Price—50 r.

One thousand years ago the Russian people saw the light of the Christian truth and the new life in the name of Christ.

For ten centuries the Russian Orthodox Church has been glorifying the Maker and delivering the redemptive sermon of the Divine teaching.

The Orthodox temple is the prayer house crowned with the Cross, the symbol of the triumph of life over death. Built by the mortals, it is the vehicle of the mystery that it shares with the Universe created by the Maker.

"The Temple is the house of the glory of Christ and the heaven on earth." The assembled believers in it are encircled with the assembled saints the holy images of which can be seen in the frescoes and icons. The Church draws its strength, fullness and power from this unity of the visible and the invisible.

The Temple is the sanctuary of the millennium-long history of the Russian Orthodox Church and Russian holiness. The Russian Church was becoming stronger and larger through the prayers and deeds of the saints, zealots and righteous men who were toiling in the name of God in Russia. Each of them was marked with the Divine Grace, each of them was a vehicle of righteousness and the best traits of the Russian national character.

Let us look back one thousand years to see how our forefathers received the Christian faith. Here is what a Russian chronicle says: "The Kievan Prince Vladimir became inspired with the thought of becoming a Christian. He stepped into the holy font and was reborn of the Spirit and water by baptising in Christ." This happened in 988 in Korsun (Chersonesus), the first of the Russian cities to be baptised in the Apostolic times.

"A large number of people gathered. Some of them went up to the neck into water, others up to the breast, some held children in their arms. The priests were praying. Vladimir rejoiced when he and his people knew God. He raised his eyes to the sky and said: 'You who created the heaven and the earth, accept these new people'." The Dnieper became the Christening font for our people. In this way the prophecy of St. Andrew came true. At the dawn of Christianity he had said of the Kievan land: "Do you see these hills? On them the grace of God will shine and a great city will appear and God will erect many churches here."

Upon adopting Christianity Russia was able to take a new, higher place in the intricate mediaeval hierarchy of states. The wealth of Byzantine Christian culture was gaining access to Christianised Russia in a new way: it was becoming part and parcel of everyday life in this country. Together with the Christian dogmas Russia got from Byzantium the eternat foundations of European culture and its Hellenist and Roman roots of which Byzantium was a custodian. Together with them Russia receieved the basic priniciples of theological and philosophical thought, the primary elements of learning, literature and the arts and the basics of law and political ideals. This was the source of the process that elevated Russia, made it responsive to the great Christian heritage. Later, when the Byzantine empire collapsed, the Moscow Kingdom was able to take the place at the head of the Orthodox world.

The St. Sophia Cathedral in Kiev with its thirteen domes was built in the early 11th century when the Kievan state was flourishing under Grand Prince Yaroslav the Wise.

Hillarion, the first Russian Metropolitan, had the following to say about the St. Sophia Cathedral in Kiev: "Yaroslav created a great and holy God's house in Kiev. It earned fame and glory among all the neighbouring peoples." It was in this cathedral that Hillarion addressed his Sermon on Grace and Order to all Orthodox believers. The cathedral was the place where the Grand Prince received ambassadors, the first library was set up there and the first Russian chronicle was written within its walls. People's assemblies gathered in front of it. Today one can see the tombs of Princess Olga and Yaroslav the Wise, the cathedral's builder, inside it.

As the first Christian churches were being built everywhere in Russia and the Orthodox faith become fairly widespread among its people the first zealots of the new faith, venerable Antonius and Theodosius of the Monastery of the Caves, appeared. They made a cave in the Kiev hill their home and lighted candles in an underground church to sing praise to God. In this way they began their feat while the Kiev-Pechery Lavra (The Kiev Monastery in the Caves) they founded was destined to become the main sacred place of the Orthodox faith in Kievan Rus.

Venerable Nestor who took monastic vows in the time of Theodosius described the monastery in the following way: "some monasteries are built with gold and silver, the monastery of Theodosius was built by his tears and prayers." Many people who abandoned the earthly kingdom for the sake of the heavenly kingdom flocked to the monastery. One of them was venerable Elijah (Ilya of Murom), the hero of Russian epic songs, who took monastic vows in the Lavra towards the end of his life. Alepius, the famous icon painter, Nestor the chronicler and twelve builders who had come from Constantinople to erect the Cathedral of the Dormition, were among its monks together with other saints and righteous men whose relics are carefully kept in the monastery.

The mighty tree of the Kievan monasticism that was known for its deeds pleasing to God and the miracles worked by its saints took root by the blessing of the Lavra's two great elders—Antonius and Theodosius. "Underground monasteries and monks appeared everywhere in our land."

For the years to come the Orthodox monasteries remained the source of divine knowledge and the focal points of spiritual life, righteousness and piety.

In monasteries everybody performs his penance on the place and in the work he is most suited to do.

An original school of icon paining and architecture that was closely associated with the Russian national character and a religious approach to measure and beauty as seen by the people was shaped in Russia.

During the earliest period of Christianity in Russia the national forms of its interpretation as realised in icon paining, architecture and sermons became evident.

As distinct from Western learning that had been thriving on the cultural and philosophical heritage of pagan Rome long before Christianity was introduced learning in Russia totally relied on the original folk wisdom and the Holy Script completed with many God-inspired works by the Fathers of the Ecumenical Orthodox Church. Unlike the West who addressed God in Latin, Russia, through the feat of Saints Cyril and Methodius, the first Slavic teachers, received the sermons and the Holy Script in its native tongue.

Learning in Russia, the intellectual and spiritual education and Christian world outlook were based on the Holy Bible and the commentaries offered by the saintly Fathers of the Orthodox Church. For many centuries has the Russian people preserved its reverence to and trust in the written word.

It was with great sorrow that the early Russian chronicles described the martyrdom of princes Boris and Gleb, the younger sons of the Kievan prince Vladimir. These first Russian saints repeated Christ's passions. They meekly and voluntarily accepted their fate of martyrs. It is on record in history that the first saints predict, as it were, the future road of their people.

In this way, the 20th century was predicted in the 10th century: during the trying years the Russian Orthodox Church and millions of its faithful followers bore their cross without complaint. The first of them saved those who came after because never the blood of Christian martyrs is shed in vain.

The feats of saints and zealots opposed the evil around them. From the very beginning they served an example of Christian meekness, patience and love. All this was especially important in the 12th century, the time of violent princely strife.

A legend says that the Sign of the Virgin icon pierced with arrows in a battle between Novgorodians and Suzdalians was flowing with blood. Yet nobody heeded the call for peace: "Why are we sowing strife everywhere, why are we pushing the Russian land to peril?".

Prince Andrei Bogolyubsky, son of Yuri Dolgoruky, was taking great pains to make his capital city of Vladimir the capital of all Russian lands. The Cathedral of the Dormition of the Holy Virgin that the pious prince erectid remains to this day the unrivaled example of church architecture. Great were the prince's plans yet short proved to be his life. The saintly and pious prince met his death at the hands of his enemies. His relics, the object of profound reverence, are kept in the Cathedral of Dormition in Vladimir.

"On the year 1237, on the third day of February, Tartars besieged the city of Vladimir and took it by storm. Many of its residents were killed without mercy or perished in fires." This is a chronicler'a account of Batu's invasion.

Like a fiery storm the Tartar-Mongol hordes swept Russia destroying her newly built cities and subjugating her principalities. The heroic all-out effort of the nation did not bring the desired results yet it was Russia that blocked the road to Europe to Batu's huge armies in 1237. Though defeated, Russia did not perish. What helped people survive? Their patience, faith and an earnest address to the Redeemer, the Holy Virgin and the saints. People were also aware of their sins. "There were loud lamentations in the city and no joy because of our sins and misdeeds; because we persisted in our sins God sent the pagans on us. He did it not as a favour for them but as a punishment for us, to divert us from our misdeeds. We all suffer from the pagan invasion sent on us by God." This nation-wide repentance bore its fruits. Prince Daniil, the youngest son of the saintly and pious Prince Alexander Nevsky, who had inherited Moscow, then one of the small Russian towns, decided to gather the disunited Russian lands together. (He was following in this great father's footsteps who had strengthened and defended the north-western Russian lands.) "I decided to do this to preserve the memory of our anscetors and our own and to keep our candle burning."

Nobody can tell how the ideas inspired by God's desire enter this world and are accepted by the worthy people who alone are able to pursue their course amid temptations and strife.

Such was the idea of saintly Metropolitan Petr who decided to shift his seat from Vladimir to Moscow. With foresight and in an anticipation of Moscow's great future the head of the Russian Church made this small town his seat in the early 14th century.

For many years Metropolitan of Moscow Alexy was carrying the heavy burden of state and church administration while Grand Prince Dimitri, his godson, was a minor. He unwearingly multiplied the forces of the Moscow Principality. Under Prince Dimitry Donskoi (canonized by the Russian Orthodox Church in 1988) Moscow became the centre that attracted all Russians. The Grand Prince was the embodiment of all the best traits of the Moscow princes: he was profoundly religious, his mind was clear and swift, he was a great soldier and a profoundly moral person in the Christian sense of the word. Venerable Sergy of Radonezh was the third providential person of that great age. History conferred on him the title of Father Superior of the Russian land.

"The Russian Orthodox soul cannot be full without venerable Sergy of Radonezh. His piety is of a special nature that differs from that of many other saints dearly loved and revered among the people. It rested on the Russian interpretation of the ideal. For him to renounce this ideal amounted to renouncing himself. In the most trying moments of our common fate every Russian heart heard his voice: 'Do not despair, my child'." (Valentin Rasputin, *The Close Light Seen from Afar*.) He was the first to set down a monastery far from all towns. In this way he initiated a new type of Russian holiness — living in wilderness. His pupils founded forty monasteries in faraway places, while their own, in turn, set up sixty more monasteries. They reached the distant corners of the Moscow Principality. Holiness was rapidly extending to cover entire Russia. The Moscow princes persisted in their efforts to gather the Russian lands around Moscow, while the monasteries' self-imposed spiritual mission united the Russian people. For many centuries people gladly accepted the monasteries and the saintly elders as their patrons capable of protecting them against injustice and the iniquitous. There were prominent figures among Sergy's followers: venerable Stephan of Perm, who enlightened the Komi and the Zyrayns, venerable Pafnuti who founded the Borovsk monastery, venerable Makary of Unzha who set up the Zheltovodsky Monastery on the Volga and the Unzha Monastery in a faraway corner of the Kostroma forests, venerable Savva Storozhevsky who laid the foundation stone of the Storozhevsky Monastery near Zvenigorod (at the western approaches to Moscow), venerable Alexander Svirsky who revived the monastery on the Isle of Valaam and venerable Zosima and Savvaty Storozhevsky, the founders of the famous Solovetsky Monastery up in the North.

On the eve of the Battle of Kulikovo Sergy, aware of the coming trials, was praying at the Trinity icon for God's help to his country. He knew beforehand that the Rissians would win. While seeing Prince Dimitry off to the battle field Sergy sent two of his monks, Peresvet and Oslyabya, with him. The battle took place on September 8, 1380, the day when the Russian Orthodox Church celebrates the Nativity of the Virgin. Two historic forces of universal significance met on the field of Kulikovo: the Russian creative force that lived according to the moral principles of Orthodoxy and the plundering Horde force who lived by violence and the philosophy of predators.

As a Russian saying goes, "God is on the side of truth not force." The Russians, reinforced by their firm faith and aware of the divine truth, defeated the horde of Mamai. This victory was of universal importance. It marked the Russian people's resurrection and made it possible for Holy Russia to return to the circle of the great powers that, according to God's design, were influencing the world historical process.

By defeating the Tartars the Moscow Principality enabled the peoples of eastern Asia who had been involved in violence and plunder by the idea of evil to regain their peaceful and creative lifestyle. They also got a chance to cooperate with Russia on the new moral principles and to become parts, at a later date, of a mighty Orthodox state.

The unquenchable icon-lamp of faith and righteousness that Sergy lit in front of the Holy Trinity icon at the moment of harsh trials is still burning. Every year, for six centuries now, a public service of thanks has been said in the Trinity-St. Sergy Lavra on St. Sergy' commemoration day.

"By the service in memory of venerable Sergy we are testing themselves," wrote Vassily Klyuchevsky, a prominent Russian historian. "By remembering him we are revising our moral stock that we inherited from the great architects of our moral order and are replenishing

it. The gates of the St. Sergy Lavra will close forever only when we would dissipate our moral heritage."

With the Tartar-Mongol yoke toppled down Russia experienced a veritable national and cultural resurrection. The Russian Orthodox Church had an active role to play in this process.

In the 14th to 16th centuries the works by the most prominent Holy Fathers and the Great Teachers of the East Christian Church were translated into Russian. Among these authors there were Vasily the Great, Gregory Nazianzus, John Climacus, Isaak of Syria and Maxim the Confessor.

This was the time when the great Russian icon-painters—Daniil Chorny, Feophanus the Greek and venerable Andrei Rublev—reached their summit. In mediaeval Russia the painter's attitude to what he was doing was determined by his Christian faith. This created a special type of the icon painter who used his art to convey his personal spiritual experience to others. There were many icon painters among the monks; in this way the painter was a kind of a vehicle of the divine will that brought us closer to the Heavenly World through the Holy Image. The act of creation was a service to God that was accompanied by strict fasting and constant prayer. When an icon was being painted in a monastery the entire brethren was fasting and praying. This alone allowed Andrei Rublev to paint his famous Trinity and the Saviour of Zvenigorod.

In the middle of the 15th century the Ecumenical Orthodox Church was confronted with the threat of a union with the Roman Church. Certain circumstances forced the Eastern hierarchs to sign the Florentine Union imposed by the Papal See. The Russian Church true to the Orthodox faith flatly rejected the union. On December 15, 1448, the Assembly of the Russian Bishops elected Jonah, the bishop of Ryazan and Murom, Metropolitan of Moscow and All Russia. It was the first independent act of the Russian Church. This was the beginning of the Russian Church's autocephalous existence. Upon the fall of the Byzantine Empire when Constantinople fell into the hands of Turks the Russian Orthodox Church remained the sole pillar of the universal Orthodoxy as the largest and the mightiest among the Orthodox Churches. "Time has come when a type of an Orthodox kingdom, the lawful heir to Byzantium, as a coming and a historically tangible reality, began to take shape in the minds of the grand princes and church writers. This awakened the thought and the feelings. Everything that the people had accumulated and loved in its collective conscience: its baptism in the name of Christ... found its way into the exceptionally rich religious and patriotic literature through the efforts of the well-read Moscow thinkers and publicist writers who mainly lived in the 15th century. In their brilliantly written works they justified the switch to the Russian land of the world-important mission of the Orthodox kingdom and the sacred significance and predistination of the Moscow statehood. With the radiant joy and the apprehension of apocalyptic responsibility they accepted and recognised this idea as a certain revelation... They pronounced their prophetic word about Holy Russia with the united heart and united voice..." (A. Kartachev, *The Fates of Holy Russia*).

The entire Russian culture of that time became the memorial of this self-consciousness. The Moscow Kremlin with its cathedrals, chambers and frescoes was the highest embodiment of this culture. The Cathedral of the Dormition, that replaced in the common Orthodox consciousness the ecumenical St. Sophia Cathedral, came to symbolise the Russian Church. "This happened in white-stoned Moscow, in Holy Russia".

"Somehow, Russian self-consciousness surged high. The grandeur of her designs showed the true nature of Russia as a cradle of world culture. At the turn of the 16th century the greatness and glory of Holy Russia was unexpectedly and splendidly revealed to the Russian soul and left an indelibile imprint on it. Russia, that has found its ideal, made great and sincere efforts to be worthy of it. If, exhausted, she fell down and sinned, she found inspiration in her ideal and raised. It was mainly the ideal that inspired her and saved her in the perilous moments of her history when life brought her at the brink of an abyss." (A. Kartashev. *The Fates of Holy Russia*).

As the elder Filofei put it, the history of Moscow, "the Third Rome" and the history of the Moscow Kingdom of the 15th and 16th centuries was the history of a unique Christian civilisation and a unique Orthodox culture that was destroyed in the 17th century by the Church schism and Peter the Great's reforms. Spiritual life of the Russian Orthodoxy was developing and added new holy images to the assemblage of the Russian saints.

Two great zealots highly revered by the Russian Orthodox Church, venerable Iosif of Volotsk and venerable Nilus of Sora, appeared in Russia at the turn of the 16th century. Venerable Iosif took monastic vows from the great elder Pafnutii of Borovsk. Upon reaching spiritual maturity he set up a monastery at the old town of Volokolamsk. Iosif introduced there a strict order. Together with the Novgorod Bishop Gennady this zealot and defender of the Orthodoxy decidedly rebuffed a heresy widespread at that time even in the Grand Prince'a family.

The 1503 Council raised the question of monasterial possessions. Venerable Joseph was a confirmed supporter of the idea of rich monasteries able to extend material help together with spiritual guidance. He himself was the best example of this. Venerable Nilus of Sora was his opponent at the Council. He and his supporters, the elders-non-possessors from a Volga monastery, insisted that "the soul for which Christ died and rose was all-important". Nilus of Sora, who initiated the teaching of non-possessors, relied on the ascetism of the Eastern Fathers of the Church. In the 16th century the cause of St. Sergy was living on in monastic life.

In the mid-16th century thirty-nine Russian saints were canonized by the efforts of Moscow Metropolitan Makary. He himself, the author of many Lives of Saints, was canonized at the 1988 Local Council, on the 1000th anniversary of the Russian Orthodox Church.

Vasily III joined other Russian lands to the Moscow Principality: Pskov, Smolensk, Ryazan and Novgorod Seversky. The Russian Church did much to promote this unity as it regarded these developments as beneficial for the Russian people and the Orthodoxy.

In 1552 Ivan the Terrible conquered the Kazan khanate, its rulers willingly accepted the Orthodoxy. The 1554 Local Council established the Kazan Diocese.

To mark his victory over the khanate Ivan the Terrible had the Cathedral of the Protection of the Virgin erected on the Red Square in Moscow. Its Moorich, Indian and Chinese domes dominated by the Russian dome convey the idea that it was Russia's task to unite different peoples and to show them the way to salvation. This was how young Ivan the Terrible formulated his aims at the beginning of his reign. At that time Russia was a rich and great courtry that amazed everybody with the variety of its life. Makary, the Moscow Metropolitan, who was the head of the Russian Church, was the closest advisor of the young tsar on all vitally important problems. It was the time when Ivan Fedorov began book-printing in Russia. The country was rapidly progressing. This peaceful development and thriving were cut short by the sudden death of Anastasia, the tsar's young wife, who was the general favourite because of her sweet nature. Terrible changes occurred in the bereaved tsar: the omnipotent *oprichnina* shrouded the Russian land in grief. During the years of trial Metropolitan Philipp was standing at the helm of the Russian Church. He alone was the support and protector for everyone, he alone was bold enough to confront the terrible tsar with opposition. Their last conversation took place in the Moscow Cathedral of the Dormition. The Metropolitan said: "Here in the cathedral we thank God for his redemption, while outside Christian blood is flowing freely. You come here to ask for absolution. You should be wise enough to absolve those who sinned against you." "You are a monk and the affairs of the state are not your concern," responded the tsar. "Yes, I am a monk. Still, I have been appointed by the Holy Spirit to become the head of the Christian Church. We together should make the welfare of and peace among the Orthodox Christians our main concern." "Keep silent, father," was the answer. "Our silence allows you to sin and is harmful for everybody... It is our duty to tell you the truth even on the pain of death".

"Do not confront my power," said the tsar. "Beware of my awe." The prelate refused to be intimidated, he continued exposing the tsar and his pernicious policies. In 1568 he was falsely accused, defrocked and exiled to the Otroch Monastery near Tver. A year later he died the death of a martyr at the hands of the scoundrel Malyuta Skuratov. His relics were first kept in the Solovetsky Monastery. Later, in 1652, under Patriarh Nikon, they were brought into the Moscow Kremlin.

Saint Kornily, the Father Superior of the Pskov-Pechery Monastery, the stronghold of the Orthodoxy in the Western Russian lands, fell victim to the tsar's iniquitous anger as well.

For four centuries now all faithful Russian people have been preserving the memory of the great martyrs. Every year the entire Russian Orthodox Church holds commemorative services.

In the 16th century, under Ivan the Terrible, the God-inspired Russian colonization of Siberia began. A chronicle from Solvychegodsk writes: "Upon saying ardent prayers the Kazaks boldly boarded their boats. The banner with the image of the Merciful Saviour that was installed in the leading boat led the Kazak detachment by marching on the water." Ermak's small troop was able to conquer the vast West Siberian lands.

"The victory is given not by many battles but by the heavenly interference". Ermak became a popular hero, his feats sang in many folk songs. Russian monks followed the Ermak army or even outstripped it.They pacified and enlightened the local pagan tribes with the Divine Word and the Cross.

During the centuries that followed numerous pagans were converted into Christianity. Prelates, righteous men and zealots were tirelessly working among them. Prelate John of Tobolsk did a lot to englighten and develop these lands. His relics are kept in the Transfiguration Cathedral of the Kremlin of Tobolsk, the old capital of Western Siberia. On his commemoration day pilgrims from all over Siberia and Russia flock to the Cathedral. Four centuries ago the bell that announced to the people of Uglich the tragic death of Prince Dimitri was exiled to Tobolsk. The age of Ivan the Terrible came to an end with the martyrdom of his younger son Prince Dimitri.

Chronicles and the frescoes in the Uglich cathedral built on the place where the young prince had been killed tell a horrifying story of his death: "'We see that you, our lord, have a new necklace,' with these words the killers approached the boy and stabbed the innocent child to death. The people rebelled and meted out their punishment on the scoundrels." Contemporaries wrote that the young prince showed great promise and that great hopes were pinned on him. With his death the Ryurik dynasty on the Russian throne ended. The historical routes of the Russian state became distorted.

The prince-martyr was canonized. Soon afterwards the Uglich tragedy resounded all over Russia with the Troubled Time and numerous sufferings of the people.

The Russian Church's spiritual elevation and the growing might of the Moscow State prompted the idea of the Patriarchate in Russia. The Russian Metropolitans of the Moscow period promoted this idea by all means at their disposal. In 1589 Metropolitan Iov was elected the first Moscow Patriarch.

In 1989 the Russian Orthodox Church solemnly marked this event. The Council of the Highest Clergy canonised Patriarch Tikhon and the first Russian Patriarch Iov.

In 1589 Iov was enthroned by the Patriarch of Constantinople Jeremy. Tsar Fedor Ioanovich, who had done much to set up a patriarchate in Russia reached an agreement with Ecumenical Patriarch Jeremy that since that time on Moscow Patriarchs would be elected by the council of the Russian bishops. At the same time, the Eastern Patriarchs in Constantinople assigned the fifth place in the hierarchy to the Russian Patriarch and recognized his rights as the head of the Autocephalous Church.

Prince Dimitri's foul murder and the sudden death of tsar Boris Godunov that followed soon afterwards are full of mysteries. The 17th century brought troubles to Russia. Famine and diseases swept the country as an ominous sign. All the man-induced elements — violence, lawlessness and lies — engulfed the country as the first pretender, the False Dimitri, invaded Russia. In the time of troubles the Patriarchs remained the bulwark of order in the country that was perishing without guidance. While earlier the Russian people used to say that they loved the Russian land as a mother loved her child, in the Time of Troubles many misguided people were prepared to sacrifice their country.

As the emenies were forcing him to crown the False Dimitri Patriarch Iov was asking the Holy Virgin to protect the Orthodoxy. He was firm in his rebuff: "I see around me our kingdom in trouble, and a triumph of lies and heresy." When the False Dimitri was killed and the relics of Prince Dimitri moved to Moscow calm and peace seemed to be close at hand.

Yet the enemies continued to disseminate rumours that the prince had been saved and was prepared to march on Moscow and take the throne provided he had enough support in the country. This was done at the time when the hopeless mother of the ill-starred prince was weeping at his coffin (earlier she had taken vows), when Iov who had gone blind and had been deposed by the traitors was lamenting the state of his country and when a new Patriarch Hermogen was calling for repentance.

At this time an army of 30,000 Polish and Lithuanian soldiers and the Russian traitors came to the Trinity-St. Sergy Lavra. Protected by its walls the defenders of the great Russian sanctuary were rebuffing the enemy attacks for sixteen months. Prayers at the Trinity icon and the relics of St. Sergy were going on day and night.

Avraamy Palitsyn, the monastery cellarer, wrote: "Everybody who were firm in their principles were executed by the enemy. The houses of God were plundered, the hearts became hardened... the minds were fogged... The native land and the Church were perishing." The Lavra defenders knew that Patriarch Hermogen had been isolated in the Chudov Monastery and was expecting his death any day. His last message to the people read: "Bless be all ready to die for the Orthodoxy." His charters inspired the Russian people to rise in defence of their native land. The Russian cities began pooling their efforts for a decisive rebuff. The Lavra remained the last stronghold of resistance. Father Superior Dionisy never abandoned his efforts to gather enough people to liberate Moscow.

In Nizhni Novgorod on the Volga, that was a rich and free city, people became inspired by the Patriarch's charter. They responded to the call of Kozma Minin Sukhoruk, the merchant head. The volunteers began their march on Moscow from Yaroslavl, from the walls of the Monastery of the Transfiguration of the Saviour. They set on the road with prayers to the Holy Virgin. The icon of the Virgin of Kazan became the symbol of liberation. Guided by the miracle-working icon and headed by Prince Dimitri Pozharsky and Kozma Minin the army entered the Kremlin on October 22, 1612. "Everywhere in Moscow people were rejoicing," wrote the chronicler. "Bells were ringing and prayers were sung. It was as if the people came out of darkness to see the light of day".

Relics of many of the prelates of the Russian Orthodox Church are kept in the Cathedral of the Dormition of the Virgin, including the relics of the saint martyr Patriarch Hermogen, the protector and the heavenly patron of Moscow, and saintly Patriarch Iov. For many centuries Moscow and Holy Russia together with it were protected by the prayers of the chosen. Through their relics the Heavenly Church inspires the Chuch on earth with divine forces. This is a great mystery.

Exhausted by the long years of troubles and bloodshed the Russian land was craving for peace and creative work. In 1619, Metropolitan Philaret, who had returned back to Russia after ten years of Polish captivity, was elected Patriarch of Moscow and All Russia. The Local Council that sat in Moscow elected his son, Mikhail Romanov, tsar of Russia. He was destined to become the founder of the Romanov dynasty on the Russian throne. His father acted as his co-ruler and closest advisor. He was also sparing no effort to restore peace and order in his native land. The 18th century brought a new style into the culture of Russia. Sumptious decorative forms took the place of earlier simplicity. Numerous splendid and great monuments were created in Novgorod, Pskov, Kostroma and Yaroslavl through the tireless efforts of saints and righteous men. They were amassing wealth rather than wasting it and people gladly donated the fruits of their labour to maintian the holy cause of creation that our Maker bequeathed on us.

Meanwhile, the Roman Union that had become a threatening cloud at the Florence Council, in the late 16th century turned into a real menace to the Orthodoxy in the South and West of Russia. A terrible storm followed. People and the staunchest of their spiritual leaders were persecuted. Lies, violence and falsehoods were freely used to make people abandon the Orthodoxy, the faith of their fathers. The Catholic rulers of Lithuania and Poland who had extended their power over these purely Slavic lands deprived the Orthodox believers of their civil rights and virtually outlawed them. Many curbed under the pressure and changed their faith. Iov, Father Superior of the Pochaevsky Monastery, who was later canonized, and other prelates called on the people at the Orthodox Council in Kiev: "Be firm in your Orthodox faith you have inherited from your fathers, remain true to it and never allow the thought of abandoning it." The Pochaevskaya Lavra in Volhinia he had founded remainden the stronghold of the Orthodoxy in the south-west of Russia. There, in the underground church, the relics of St. Iov are kept. The monastery and

its Father Superior extended its help and protection to all Orthodox believers who found themselves under Catholic rule and were persecuted for their faith.

In the mid-17th century persecution by the Jesuites and the Uniates and temptations of the Protestants were discontinued. Tsar Alexei Mikhailovich spread his rule first to Smaller (the Ukraine) and then Belaya (Byelorussia) Russia. The Russian land that remained divided because ot the tragic circumstances reunited under the aegis of one state and one church. Patriarch Nikon (1652-1658) did much to make this reunification possible.

The new Moscow Patriarch came from a peasant family that lived on the Volga near Nizhni Novgorod. His exceptional abilities, strong will and sharp mind earned him the place of the tsar's closest friend. The courtiers were disappointed and irritated. A gifted architect and thinker who was constantly seeking true knowledge Patriarch Nikon set up New Jerusalem not far from Moscow, on the banks of the river Istra. Meanwhile, the Monastery Department accountable to the tsar began interfering in the Church affairs according to the new Council Decisions. This was an unprecedented development and it was regarded as an unwelcome interference.

The Patriarch's enemies were inciting the tsar against the country's spiritual leader: "He has stirred up the entire country and trampled down your authority. Nobody is listening to you any longer. He alone is the source of all trouble."

The Patriarch retorted: "His Majesty has extended its rule over the Church contrary to the Divine designs. He even wants to shield God himself with the wings of his eagle." The tsar had already taken a firm decision to depose Nikon with the help of the Eastern Patriarchs. At the council that followed he was accused of despotism; it was said that his removal from the capital had bred temptations and schisms. He rejected all accusations and pointed out that his judges were not sincere. Nevertheless, he was stripped of his position and sent to a monastery as a simple monk.

Patriarch Nikon had initiated a revision of the Church books according to the Greek originals to fortify the unity of the Ecumenical Orthodoxy in Russia. The old rites were forbidden. (The bans were lifted in 1971 at the Local Council of the Russian Orthodox Church.) Many people rejected the novelties being suspicious that the Patriarch was biased to Rome. They rejected outright the efforts to push into oblivion the old Russian rites inherited from the many generations of Orthodox ancestors, prelates and zealots. Violence applied by the state to the unwilling made the latter even more eager to suffer for the just cause. This became the meaning of life of many people: Archpriest Avvakum, a fiery preacher and author of the brilliant *Pustozersk Collection*, the monks of the Solovetsky Monastery who were defending their cloister for eight years, the famous *Boyarynya Morozova*, and many other less illustrous personalities. A fair part of the believers, and perhaps the best part of them, supported the scismatics. Nobody can tell how many of them sacrificed their lives by setting fire on themselves. The scism was a tragedy, not limited to the Church. It was a great national tragedy.

Patriarch Nikon fell victim to the intrigues, though his towering figure detracted attention from those who sought to weaken the Russian Orthodox Church and the Russian State. The next blow came when the Church was deprived of the Patriarchate under Peter the Great. For more than a century the Russian religious boat was firmly guided by the patriarchs. They defended the Church's independence in the face of the earthly powers and argues its interests before the tsar. The believers held the Patriarch higher than the political and secular powers. Peter the Great's reforms dealt a deathly blow to the centuries-old traditions and fortified absolutism. When in 1700 Patriarch Adrian died the emperor prevented the elections of a new patriarch being apprehensive, not without grounds, that the new spiritual leader of his subjects might resist his innovations and reforms. In 1721, he set up Collegium for Spiritual Affiars in St. Petersburg, his new capital. Soon it was transformed into the Holy Synod of which the highest clergy were the members. A secular official appointed by the Emperor, the ober-procurator, held the key post. This was an undisguised interference into the affairs of the Church. This new period in the history of the Russian Orthodox Church was called the Synodal period.

In the 18th century many great zealots were active and achieved the state of sanctity. Metropolitan Dimitri of Rostov was one of the best educated people of his time. He revised the collection of the *Lives of the Russian Saints*, the most-read book of the Orthodox world. Tikhon Zadonsky spared no effort to reassure those who slackened in their faith: "It happens sometimes that while many are working together one is idling on the side. Somebody is sure to ask him: 'Why are you staying aside?' In the same way one should encourage a believer who has weakened in his faith: 'All the Christians are fulling their duty. Why aren't you?'."

Prelate Mitrofani of Voronezh taught: "Any man should follow the rule of the sages: work and know measure and you will grow rich; drink and eat little and you will be healthy; do good, refrain from evil and you will be saved."

Through the fault of the Synod prelate Innokenty of Irkutsk did not get his payment till his dying day. Still, he bore the hadships uncomplainingly. As a good pastor he was constantly extending his bishopric. By the end of his life it included the Yakutsk and Ilim regions.

In the 18th century the Russian Orthodox Church considerably stepped up its inner and outer missionary activity. Orthodox missions appeared in Siberia, the Far East, Japan, China and Korea, The venerable Herman of Alaska, a humble monk of the Valaam monastery, canonized in 1970, brought the light of the Orthodox faith on the North American continent. He baptised Aleutians on the Aleutian Islands and Alaska. He was the only missionary who stayed behind on the island of Kodyak with the people whom he had baptised and who were holding him in high esteem. The zealot who was preaching self-sacrifice and non-possessing used to say: "I am a humble servant and a nurse of the people who live here." His relics are kept in the Cathedral of Resurrection on the island of Kodyak.

Prelate Innokenty (Veniaminov) who was later appointed Metropolitan of Moscow, was justly called the Apostle of America and Siberia. He brought the Orthodox faith to tens of thousands of people, created an Aleutian alphabet and grammar and translated the Gospels into this language.

For two centuries already the Russian Church is thriving in America. In 1970 it became Autocephalous.

It was precusely in the 18th century that post-Petrine society, its enlightened strata mainly consisting of the gentry, was gradually abandoning the Church. They learned to despise the Orthodoxy as something backward that prevented them from assimilating the Western lifestyle and world view. However, an encounter with the Western philosophy bred disillusionment and disrespect to everything Russian in the upper crust and drove it to other countries in search for ideals.

Since the time of Nilus of Sora and the elders-non-possessors the spiritual monastic life was declining amid prolonged troubles. In the late 18th century, however, a mysterious shift occurred: spiritual ties connected Mt. Athos and Moldavia, one of the suffering parts of Russia. Paisi Velichkovski, a Moldavian elder, who set up a small St. Elijah monastery on Mt. Athos, a great zealot who translated works of the Holy Fathers into Slavonic, revived the old traditions of a clever and heartfelt player. His writings produced a great impression on all Russian monasteries.

At the turn of the 19th century a zealot who had accepted a monastic name of Seraphim (fiery) appeared in the Sarov monastery in the impenetrable Tambov forests. His monastic feat cannot be rivalled—for more than thirty years he lived as a hermit, he spent one thousand nights praying while standing on a stone. "The meaning of life'" taught he, "is in seeking the Divine Spirit, the 'breath of live' that alone placed man above all other creatures and made him similar to God." St. Seraphim is one of those holy men who are especially liked by the Russian people. "We rever them not only as the heavenly patrons of Holy and sinful Rissia: in them we are looking for spiritual guidance. The entire country lighted their icon lamps at their fire." (Vasily Klyuchevski).

According to a legend the holy elder used to tell his pupils that as he was rising in his prayer he saw the Russian land shrouded in a bluish mist of the prayers sent up to God by the God-fearing and hard-working peasants. The country was fleely and joyfullly breathing with these prayers that linked her to the life-giving Heavenly world. At those times, however, at the age of Pushkin and the Decembrists, the spiritual poison the occult lodges of high society were steadily emanating contaminated Russia's aura of faith. This revealed to the holy prophet the tragic events that were in store for Russia in one hundred years' time.

The 19th century was rich in those who embodied the Russian holiness, the traditions of spiritual councelling and righteousness. Bishop Ignaty (Bryanchaninov), Bishop Feofan the Recluse, St. Ksenia of St. Petersburg, the elders of the Optina Monastery and many other zealots, some of them known to every Russian, others not known to anybody were daily carrying on their feat of serving God and people.

The Russian Orthodox Church made its weighty contribution to Russia's triumph over Napoleon in 1812. One hundred and fifty years later the prayer for the victory of the Russian army composed by Archbishop Augustin Vinogradsky and sang at Borodino in September 1812 was said in all Russian churches during the Great Patriotic War of 1941-1945.

The Church history termed the 19th century the Age of Filaret. Metropolitan of Moscow Filaret, an outstanding theologian and preacher and a genuine ascetic, was the spiritual teacher of the entire country. Through his efforts a vast Gethemane *skit* (an auxilary monastery) was set up at the Trinity-St. Sergy Lavra. The Optina Monastery in the Kaluga diocese was flourishing under his patronship. Gogol, the great Russian writer, recounted: "Even before you reach the monastery, you can feel its influence. The nature and men become more welcoming, the bows lower and an interest in man greater. On my way I turned into the monastery and the impression will stay with me forever. Never have I seen similar brothers. There was no need to ask them about their life—their faces spoke for them".

For a century the Optina Monastery remained the focal point of Russia's spiritual and intellectual life. The tradition of elders that was, in fact, the tradition of spiritual guidance and councelling, made the monastery famous. The long line of the great Optina elders was started with hieromonk Lev (Leonid) whose soul was flowing with love and pity. He used to say: "Many, especially among the common people, perish because of their ignorance and spiritual feebleness. Now can I disregard their spiritual feebleness. How can I disregard their spiritual needs?" Hieromonk Makary carried on the great task initiated by Paisy Velichkovsky. Works by the Holy Fathers and Teachers of the Church appeared through his incessant efforts and cares. "We should abandon European customs," wrote he, "for the love of Holy Russia... be firm in the Orthodox faith and repent the past".

All Russian people knew about the kind father elder Amvrosy (canonised by the 1988 Local Council). Thousands upon thosands flocked to him in search of salvation. "I see that yours is a hard lot, that you do not know how to live and why," he said to those who came to speak to him. "Indeed, how should one live? One should live without cares, one should not condemn anybody or be a nuisance to anyone, and show respect to all." He firmly believed that in every human soul, bereaved found solace, exasperated became pacified.

The traditions and experience of spiritual guidance were transferred from the teachers to their pupils in the Optina Monastery.

It attracted people from all walks of life: peasants, famous writers and scientists came to meet the elders, ask a blessing from them and listen to their wise words. The importance of this phenomenon cannot be overestimated: the elders returned the Russian educated classes to the bosom of the Russian Orthodox Church. Professors of higher educational establishments, the best writers, philosophers and journalists came to the monastery is search of spiritual advice. Among them were Nikolai Gogol, the Kirieyevski brothers, Prof. Shevyrev, Fedor Dostoevsky, Grand Prince Konstantin Konstantinovich, Vasily Rozanov and Leontiev.

Nunneries guided by holy elders Makary and Leonid revived their activity under the influence of the Optina Monastery and the example set earlier by the venerable Seraphim who had provided spiritual guidance to the Diveev nunnery. On the in intiative of elder Amvrosy the famous Shamordono nunnery near Kazan was set up. It reached its peak under Mother Superior Sophia when an orphanage and school for girls were set up, together with a hospital and house for elderly and disabled women, an icon painting shop and a printshop. Many other nunneries imitated this example.

Throughout the 19th century the Optina Monastery was the magnet that attracted all the best spirit-guided minds of Russia. The Kirieyevski brothers, the spiritual sons of the Optina elders, helped them in their educational efforts. Peter Kirieyevski wrote that they were convinced that "the national life is full-blooded where the traditions are respected." These secular zealots and righteous men joined forces with Khomyakov and other like-minded people from among the Slavophiles to turn public consciousness back to the Church and the Christian dogmas of love, since "there is no loftier love than laying down one's soul for one's friend." The Russian Orthodox people was acting according to this commandement during the Russian-Turkish war (1877-1878) by suffering great losses in the name of the liberation of the Bulgarian people, its brother in the Orthodox faith. In Russia this feat caused an unprecedented upsurge of historical and national consciousness. It was not a mere coincidence that precisely at that time monumental Cathedral of Christ the Saviour was built in Moscow as a national prayer. Erected on voluntary donations the cathedral was painted by the foremost Russian painters. It was dedicated to the memory of those who died in the Patriotic War of 1812. Everyone could read the fiery words of the Appeal to the Russian Nation issued in 1812 and exhibited in the cathedral: "Every nobleman should become Prince Pozharsky, every priest Avraamy Palitsyn, every commoner Minin. The noble gentry, at the times of danger you invariably came to save the Motherland. Holy Synod and the clergy! You have always prayed for Rissia's wellbeing. The Russian people! The brave descendants of the brave Slavs! Many times in the past you defeated those who came armed onto your land. Unite with the cross in your heart and the sword in your arm. You will be invinsible! " This monumental cathedral that was the prayer to Christ, the memory of the nation and one of the most splendid landmarks of Moscow and the entire country was destroyed in the early thirties together with many other Moscow churches and monasteries.

Theology and theological education were flourishing in the 19th century. Metropolitan Platon Levshin opened a new page in the history of theological enlightenment and education. He transformed the old Slavic-Graeko-Latin Academy and moved it to the Trinity-St. Sergy Lavra where it survived till our time. In 1809 a new theological academy was opened in St. Petersburg, ten years later the old Kievan academy, founded in the early 18th century, was reopened. The Kazan Theological Academy was specialising in training Orthodox missionaries. The Russian theological schools did a lot to enlighten and educate the people. They raised a splening cohort of prominent church figures, scholars, theologians and historians who enjoyed world fame.

As it was drawing to its end the 19th century left to the coming 20th century the ideas of conciliarism, seeking the truth in Christianity and the ideals of Holy Russia as embodied by the best Orthodox minds of the country. The Russian Orthodox Church met the new century at the crest of its spiritual and creative potential. Though the upper educated crust was inclined towards atheism, the Western secular values and detrimental West European mysticism, the healthy forces survived in Russia both in the upper circles and among the common people. They drew force from the Orthodox traditions of the Russian religious life that went back to the Slavs and Byzantium. The holy image of Orthodoxy never faded in the minds and souls of the Russians. Religious processions with miracle-working icons of the Holy Virgin—of Kazan, Vladimir, Smolensk, Tikhvin, Kursk-Korennaya, Kaluga and others—attracted many devotees. Monasteries and nunneries were alive with the wisdom and prayers of elders and zealots. Hunderds of thousands of laymen, both men and women songht their blissing, prayers, advice and consolation by making their confessions to them.

In 1903, canonization of St. Seraphim turned into a country-wide festival. People preserved his deeds and his life in their memory. When Seraphim of Sarov returned to his monastery after thirty years of life as a hermit people came to see him in an endless stream. "Christ has risen", were his words addressed to everyone. He extended his welcome to everyone be it a righteous man or a robber and greeted everyone with a low bow. He returned their divine likeness to those who had sinned and had been lost on the earthy way. Upon his canonization his healing love was protecting the entire country. God knows that Russia was badly needing it in the face of the coming grim trials.

Souls of hundreds of thousands of believers were enveloped in their individual profoundly religious feeling. The Russian Church, however, as a single unit, was unable to make its voice heard. It was deprived of the right to offer its opinion on what was going on in the country. Father Ioann of Kronstadt, the highest spiritual authority of the time, whose fame as a miracle-worker and a righteous man travelled across the borders of Russia, said: "Why were not we entitled to the help from the Heavenly Church, Christ and the Holy Virgin, and the saints in the war with Japan? Because many Russians, especially from among the intellectuals, have disrupted the union with the Heaven through disbelief, malice, blasphemy, pride, depravity, robbery, murder and inobedience to power and parents. When the unity with God had been disrupted, the Heaven withdrew its help and the Holy Virgin no longer shows us her protection." He warned the Russian people: "Lately, the Russian kingdom has become the kingdom of unheard-of and spontaneous terrors — the rebelled scoundrels are laying waste the Russian land and 'the wicked men threaten to seize the thrones of the powerful' and take their place . What would have happened to Russia if these 'rulers' succeeded? Do not forget that they are enemies of Russia and the Orthodox faith who are seeking to deprive the Church of its rightful beauty, its God-inspired Service, its property and its freedom. They want to shackle the Russians and their faith and to impose on them their own 'beliefs'. The intellectuals who have lost the faith of their fathers through their thoughtlessness offer a pitiful show. They have lost the faith on which our life is based in the time of troubles, which is our sheet-anchor amid the misfortunes that befell our Motherland" (Sermon of October 21, 1906).

At the turn of the 20th century Archbishop Nikon of Vologda began publishing the famous *Troitsa Sheets* in the Trinity-St. Sergy Lavra in millions of copies and other larger editions that were extremely popular throughout the country. The Pochaevskaya Lavra issued its own newspaper. Other publishing firms followed suit: the Russian Pilgrim, Tuzov's firm, the Soul Saving Reading, the Helmsman, the Faith and the Reason and others. *Diocese News* appeared in every large administrative units on par with secular newspapers.

This shows that people were awakening to their Christian existence and were eager to take guidance so that to organise it in the correct way. The idea of convening a Local Council with the aim of reestablishing the Patriarchate in Russia was gaining currency through the concerted efforts of all Othodox believers. This idea first appeared during the reign of Emperor Alexander III who tried to return his country onto her specifically national road. Many of his subjects began looking back at the Motherland's past and the idea of the Patriarch as the head of the Russian Church. Metropolitan Antony (Vadkovsky) was an active defender of this idea. While the rector of St. Petersburg Theological Academy he was zealously promoting among the students the idea of the Russian Church's liberation from the state domination and the return to the patriarchate. Archimandrite Mikhail (Gribanovsky) and Metropolitan Antony (Khrapovitsky) were actively supporting Metropolitan Antony (Vadkovsky). By the middle of the reign of Tsar Nicholai II (who himself keenly felt the values of mediaeval Russia) the idea of the patriarchate in Russia had been commonly accepted. At its meeting on March 22, 1905, the Holy Synod unanimously agreed to submit its report on the reinstatement of the patriarchate to the tsar and to convene the All-Russian Church Council. A year later a preliminary body gathered that included the highest hierarchs, the most respected professors of theology, prominent specialists in the affiars of the Church and political figures. They sat down to elaborate the concrete steps. The forthcoming church reforms drew much interest of the public. The wide discussions of these problems intensified the religious awarenese in the Russian people. The 1912 preparatory council was another step towards the practical implementation of the reforms. The First World War that broke out unexpectedly postponed them for an indefinite period. Russia was at the threshold of the most tragic period of its millennium-long history. The initial failures, the perish of the huge army of General Samsonov in Poland bled the country white and weakened the mighty and rich power Russia had been on the eve of the war. Defeated on the fronts and torn apart by treason and dissent at home the country strained its efforts to stay afloat. The best among the best — officers and soldiers — were dying for God, Russia and the tsar. The February coup stroke when the situation at the fronts had stabilised and the victory was near at hand. "I see everywhere nothing but treason, cowardice and deceit," the tsar wrote in his journal on March 2, 1917, when he had been forced to abdicate. With the destruction of the core the country was rapidly disintegrating. On the same day, March 2, 1917, a holy image of the Virgin known everywhere as the Powerful was discovered in a miraculous way in the old village of Kolomenskoe not far from Moscow. In this way Our Lord showed whom the tsar handed over his Orthodox power.

To attract the clergy and the believers (who at that time made up the bulk of the country's population) the Provisional Government consented to convene the All-Russian Council that had already been prepared. It was opened on August 15, 1917, with a solemn service in the Cathedral of the Dormition in the Moscow Kremlin. Let us turn to what an eye-witness had to say about this signal event. Metropolitan Anastasius wrote his memoirs in exile half a century later. "When it was decided to convene the Council many were rightly apprehensive lest it would be carried away with the revolutionary storm that might weaken the Church's authority. Nothing of the kind happened... The 1917 Council united the best and the staunchest defenders of the Church from all walks of life. They came with the already formulated decision to reestablish the Patriarchate... Here the conciliarism that alone could help the truth triumph came out with a great force. Everyone, be it a wise theologian with his vast stock of knowledge and a wide spiritual horizon, a secular scholar with his disciplined mind, a public figure who knew how to bring the opposing sides together and to reconcile them, a peasant endowed with common sense and a simple faith that rejected all temptations, a humble monk with his profound spiritual experience, a bishop and a priest with their gift for enlightenment, all of them were united into a single body by an Apostolic word supplementing, as it were, each other and presenting, together, the complete set of talents and knowledge indispensable for the authoritative Local Council. As it was being discussed at the council the idea of the Patriarchate was gradually becoming clearer and was gaining more supporters... The canonade of the Bolshevik guns trained on the Kremlin was the loudest and the weightiest argument in its favour. Destruction evident everywhere endangered the very existence of Russia. Those who were not deceived by the temptations of a revolution were striving with their hearts towards the integrity and unity of their native land. They sought to preserve its spiritual image intact. This could not be done outside the Church that many times in the past resurrected the disintegrating Russian state and popular organism with its life-giving spirit. "October 31, 1917 is a significant date in the history of the Russian Church. On that day the Holy Synod was abolished and three candidates on the throne of Iov and Hermogen were nominated. They were Archbishop of Kharkov Antonius, Archbishop of Novgorod Arseny and Metropolitan of Moscow Tikhon. Everyone was aware that the burden of the future head of the Church would be an exceedingly heavy one. It seems that the natural abilities and human strength would prove inadequate in this situation. This explains why the bishops, the majority of the clergy and the laymen present at the Council were reluctant to shoulder the responsibility of the choice. The moment was crucial, everybody felt that the Heavenly Helmsman Himself would interfere and point to the man He was entrusting with the helm of the Russian Church in the turbulent time.

"Elections were fixed for Sunday, November 5 after a liturgy in the Cathedral of Christ the Saviour. Metropolitan Tikhon was calm and composed, never abandoning his usual bonhomie. When seeing the Council participants off to the Cathedral (the candidates were forbidden to be present at the election ceremony) he said: 'Do your duty. Here I shall attend the service, have my dinner and lie down to rest". This was not a joke: the Metropolitan was not craving for power and was the calmest of the three candidates. When still a student he earned a nickmane of a patriarch among his friends. His dead mother came to her ill husband in his dream to predict that their son Vasily would be 'great'.

"The cathedral was overflowing with those who came to ask God to reveal His will to the Russian Church. After a liturgy and a short prayer elder Alexy from the Zosima Monastery drew out one of the three notes placed in a vessel in front of the icon of the Holy Virgin of Vladimir. He opened it and declared in a loud and solemn voice: 'Metropolitan of Moscow Tikhon'. Immediately all those present fell that the burden was lifted from their heart. 'This is the Divine Will', 'He was selected by the Virgin' the people were saying each other. The happy faces and calmness showed that the Patriarch was to the heart of his people. The prayers that followed thanked God for His divine interference and the satisfaction of the entire Church that acquired the head.

"The Council decided to ask the new power for a permission to use the Dormition Cathedral in the Moscow Kremlin for a solemn service and the crowning of the newly elected Patriarch. The detailed descriptions of the old rites and of the ceremonies used on the similar occasions in the past were carefully studied. To add significance to the forthcoming ceremony it was decided to use the old precious things from the Patriarch's stores. Early in the morning of November 21 the bishops, clergy and other members of the council came to the Troitskie gate of the Kremlin to meet Tikhon. Greeted with due honours he entered the cathedral full of people. The sumptuous service that followed showed that Moscow was preserving its grandeur it was famous for since time immemorial.

"History itself was witnessing the ceremony. The sacred bonds disrupted by Peter the Great's impassionate hand were being tied together. The Patriarch, clad in the cloths of Nikon and Adrian and holding St. Peter's staff in his hands, came out to the people as an amazing picture of the old time. One felt that Russia herself was embodied by the Holy Council—the Metropolitans, Archbishops, Bishops, Archimandrites, monks and the laymen from all walks of life, noble princes and commoners. All of them were rejoicing like children who knew that their father had returned to them. All of them were aware that the poitiff they had elected was, in fact, being sacrificed for the sins of the fallen people. The vacant tsar's place just opposite the Patriarch's throne was another eloquent reminder. All the hearts were heavy with foreboding. Everybody felt that great trials were in store for the Church and its newly elected head because it alone was standing unwaveringly amid the raging revolutionary storm and it alone was showing resistance to the madness that has enveloped the people."

The foreboding came true. Many of the Council participants were to die the death of a martyr.

Patriarch Tikhon was to shoulder the burden of leading the Church through the hardships of the Civil War, the famine, dissent inside the clergy and unprecedented persecution of the Orthodox Church and the faithful believers. "There were many saintly prelates, righteous men and God's fools in Russia. Yet so far there were few martyrs. The saintly martyr whose blood went to the roots of Christianity throughout the world and that was daily praised by the earthly Chirch was practically unknown in the Heavenly Russian Church. The time has come to augment their ranks. The few martyrs of the past are now joined by a great number of new martyrs. The crowned tsar and his family were the first victims to be followed by Vladimir, Metropolitan of Kiev, who was a namesake of Saint Prince Vladimir, other hierarchs, princes, boyars, soldiers, monks, scientists and common people, town dwellers and villagers, nobles and ordinary people. The new martyrs appeared in all corners of the vast country and they came from all walks of life. The country was drenched in their bloood and was blessed with it." (Archbishop Ioann Maximovich).

In February 1917, during the fist days of the revolution, Anatoly, one of the last elders from the Optina monastery, described Russia's future in prophetic terms: "There will be a storm. The Russian boat will be destroyed. Some people will survive on its remnants. Not all of them perish. Everyone should repent and pray ardently". The Saintly Patriarch of Moscow and All Russia was the great patron of the entire suffering Orthodox people during the most trying years. Patriarch Tikhon died in 1925 while fulfilling his duty to the Church and the people. The 1988 Council canonised Job, the first Russian Patriarch, and Patriarch Tikhon. Separated by several centuries they were destined to become the bulwark of the doomed Motherland perishing in the fratricidal war.

In the twenties and thirties all the monasteries were closed; several churches were functioning in the country where before the revolution there were tens of thousands; believers were persecuted. The greater part of bishops were executed, others were imprisoned or exiled. The Church found itself in a difficult situaion. Upon the death of Patriarch Tikhon, Metropolitan Sergy, the locum tenens, stood at the head of the Russian Orthodox Church. He spared no effort to protect the Church against complete destruction. Together with the Church and the faithful believers he weathered another grim trial—the Great Patriotic War—when the Church was straining its spiritual and material forces to help the country. Patriarch Sergy, elected in 1944, and Patriarch Alexy, who was standing at the helm for a quarter of a century, had to shoulder the troubles of the post-war recovery. Still, protected by the Holy Virgin, the light of the Church was never extinquished, the prayer never stopped and the life inside the Church continued.

Upon the death of Patriarch Alexy in 1971, Patriarch Pimen was elected at the Local Council of the Russian Orthodox Church. He led the increased and fortified Church to its millennium. The festivities were opened in June 1988 with a Local Council of the Russian Orthodox Church at which nine saints were canonised, a new charter adopted and various sides of the Church's inner life discussed in detail. The new situation in the country proved to be favourable for the Church as well: the entire country took part in the jubilee festivities.

On May 4, 1990, Patriarch of Moscow and All Russia Pimen died and was buried in the Cathedral of the Dormition of the Trinity-St. Sergy Lavra, of which he, like all other Russian Patriarchs before him, was the Archimandrite.

The Russian Church has gone through its millennium-long history with flying colours. Today, as before it is firm in its faith, dedicated to its ideals of peace and believes that God and the Virgin will never abandon it and that "there will be a great divine miracle and all the fragments will reunite by the Divine will. The boat will be recreated to its former grandeur and will continue its route charted by God. It always remembers the words of its Heavenly Founder and Redeemer Christ: 'I will build my church; and the gates of hell shall not prevail against it'" (Mat. 16:18).

Crucifixion. Icon of the 15th
century

16

"O Christ our God, good builder of Thy Father's house, we assume Thy holy cross, on which Thou shonest to the world like a luminary, and sing to Thee: blessed is God's Lamb, Who hath brought eternal salvation to the world, for all ages to come."

"O God our Father, this is Thy beloved Son... I sing to Him, Who died for my sake: Every toung and every tribe hath been redeemed with His blood, sing the Lord's praises and exalt Him ever."

(Canon of Christ's Passion)

"O Christ our God, wondrous and unfathomable font of mercy, Who prayedst for Thy enemies the crucifiers to God the Father, grant that I, a sinner, also may have the grace of loving my enemies..."

Descent from the Cross. Icon of
the 15th century

18

O Lord Jesus Christ, Son of the Living God, O Creator of Heaven and Earth, Saviour of the world, behold me, an unworthy one and the most execrable sinner, humbly kneeling in my heart before the glory of Thy majesty, I hymn the Cross and Thy sufferings and give thanks to Thee, God and King of all, Who hast graciously assumed all the toil, and misfortunes, and afflictions, and sufferings that are man's lot. Share in all our sorrows, needs, and bitternesses as our Helper and Saviour. Almighty Master, Thou needest none of This but for the deliverance of mankind, and Thou enduredst the cross and the torment to redeem us all in the face of the cruel designs of the enemy. O Lover of mankind, who hast suffered for all and for me, a sinner, I have no knowledge of what I can give Thee in return: for both my soul and my body derive from Thy grace, and all mine are Thine, and I am Thine.

O gracious Lord, I place all my hope in Thy infinite mercy, I sing to Thy unspeakable long-suffering, I magnify Thy immeasurable kindness, I worship Thy Most-Pure Passion and, lovingly kissing Thy sores, I cry out: have mercy on me, a sinner, and grant that Thy Holy Cross should not be barren in me, and that, sharing here as I do in Thy suffering with faith, I should be vouchsafed also to witness the glory of Thy Kingdom in Heaven. Amen.

(Prayer to the Crucified Lord Jesus)

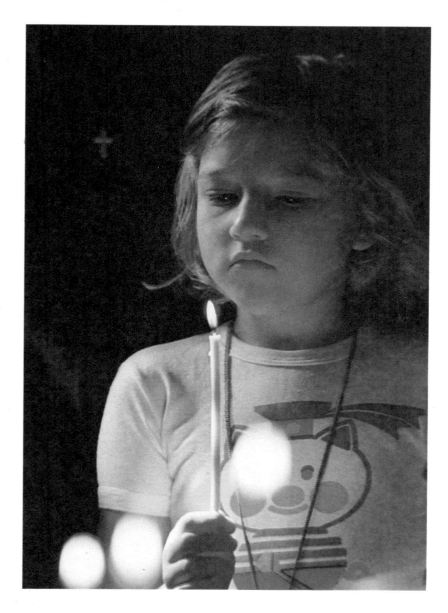

The Laying of Christ's Body in
the Tomb. Icon of the 15th
century

O genuine Sun of Truth descending into the coffin, as the Most Pure Virgin, stricken with maternal grief, burns by Thy Cross with love of Thee like a luminous candle, receive our hearts' prayers with Hers: O Jesus, Who hast risen to the cross, raise us, the fallen ones, to Thy father; O Jesus, Who wast given an Eternal Virgin for a Mother, teach us virginity and purity. O Jesus, Who entrustedst a pupil of Theology to Her that gave birth to God's Word, entrust us too to Her Maternal protection; O Jesus, Conqueror of the world and hell, vanquish the unbelief, the worldly pride and the eyes' lust that abide in us. O Jesus, destroyer of the realm of death, save me from eternal death; O Jesus, God's Son, remember us when Thou comest in Thy Kingdom.

(Acathistos to Christ's Divine Passion Ikos 11.)

Resurrection of Christ. Icon by
monk Zenon, the 1980s

"O resurrected King Jesus Christ, our Saviour, Who hast descended to the nether regions and destroyed the eternal bonds that held our souls constrained, release me from the bonds of sin. I cry out to Thee thus: O Jesus, Who entrustedst Thy beloved pupil to Thy Mother, entrust me too to Her salvific custody. O Jesus, Who turnedst the suffering of Thy Mother into joy, grant that I, a cursed one, may bear my cross with patience; O Jesus, Who hast given the world Thy Mother for a Protectress, grant that I, a sinner, may find myself under her shelter; O Jesus, Who didst not forbid children to touch Thee, give me their mildness; O Jesus, Who speakest to the harlot, "Go hence and sin no more", vouchsafe that I shall not anger Thee. O resurrected Christ, resurrect our souls".

(Acathistos to Christ's Resurrection, ikos 10)

Christ Pantocrator. Fresco by
Dionisy. 1502—1503 (a copy)

For every man the Divine Word reveals the hidden meaning of life.
"I am the light of the world: he that followeth me shall not walk in darkness, but shall have the light of life" (Jn. 8—12).

"The Baptism of Russ is the day of spiritual birth of the Orthodox Russian people. The Baptism of Russ is a day when the Russian Orthodox Church was historically born. The Baptism of Russ marked the beginning of the history of Holy Russia" (from a speech by Metropolitan Filaret, the Patriarchal Exarch to All the Ukraine).

Gospel of the
Altar

Baptism of Russ. Icon by
monk Zenon. 1988

24

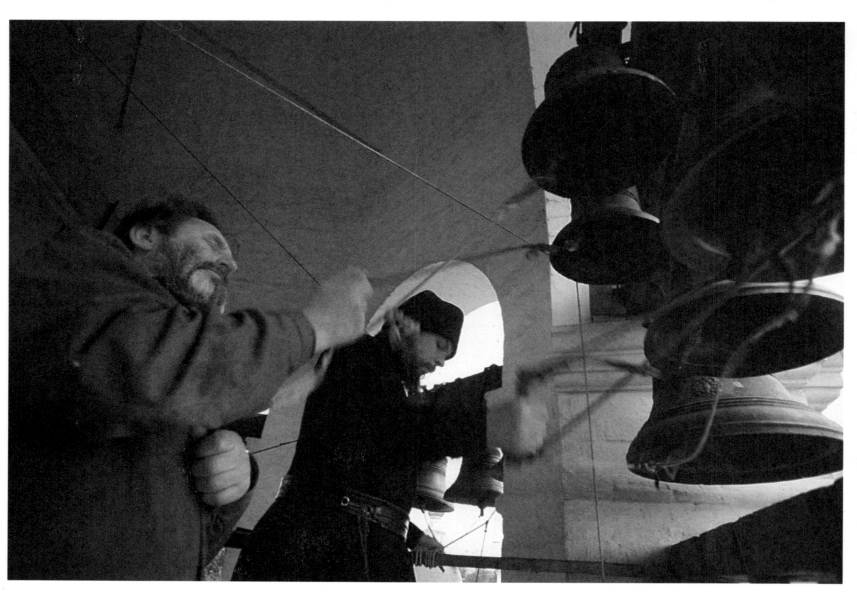

Just like one thousand and one hundred years ago the Churches of God' invite all the Orthodox believers for salvific prayers.

PRAYER TO ALL THE SAINTS
OF THE LAND OF RUSSIA

O all-blessed God's saints
wise-in-God, ye that have
sanctified the Land of Russia
with your feats of asceticism,
that have left your bodies
in her soil like seeds of faith,
that confront God's Throne
with your souls and pray
for her untiringly.
On this common feast of yours,
we, your sinful brethren,
make bold to, raise
this eulogy to ye.
Christ's spiritual warriors,
ye have finally vanquished
the foe with your patience
and courage and redeemed
us from his temptations
and snares.
We praise your great exploits.
God's beacons pouring
forth the light of faith
and virtue and illuminating
our minds and hearts
with the knowledge of God,
we extol your saintly living.
Heavenly flowers that have
blossomed beautifully
in our northern land,
spreading the fragrance
of gifts and miracles
in every quarter, we glorify
your great works.

Our intercessors and protectors,
we laud your God-like love,
we put our trust in your help,
we fall down before ye
and cry out: our saintly
relatives, all of ye
that have shone forth since
olden times or lived recently,
manifest or concealed,
known or unknown!
Remember our weakness
and humility and pray to Christ
our God that we may
safely cross the ocean
of life and preserve intact
the treasure of faith,
that we may reach the harbour
of eternal salvation and,
through the grace and love
of the Saviour, our Lord
Jesus Christ, settle
in the blessed abodes
of our Heavenly home
land with ye and all the saints
that have pleased Him
since the beginning of time.
To Him and His Eternal Father
and the Holy Spirit,
unceasing praise and worship
by all creatures is due
in ages of ages.
Amen.

The Partiarch of Moscow and All Russia Pimen blesses the believers of the one — thousand — year-old Russian Orthodox Church in the Trinity — St.Sergy Lavra.

Filaret, Metropolitan of Kiev and Galicia, the Patriarchal Exarch to All the Ukraine, a permanent member of the Holy Synod

Vladimir, Metropolitan of Rostov and Novocherkassk, the Patriarchal Exarch to Western Europe, Chancellor of the Moscow Patriarchate, a permanent member of the Holy Synod

Filaret, Metropolitan of Minsk and Grodno, the Patriarchal Exarch to Byelorussia, a permanent member of the Holy Synod

His Holiness the Patriarch of Moscow and All Russia heads the Russian Orthodox Church and guides it together with the Holy Synod

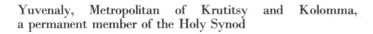

Yuvenaly, Metropolitan of Krutitsy and Kolomma, a permanent member of the Holy Synod

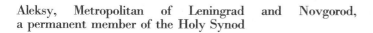

Aleksy, Metropolitan of Leningrad and Novgorod, a permanent member of the Holy Synod

"Thou shalt love the Lord thy God with all thy heart, and with all thy soul, and with all thy strength, and with all thy mind; and thy neighbour as thyself" (Luke 10:27).

The Icon of Our Lord Jesus Christ "Not-Made-by-Hands", 12th century, the Dormition Cathedral, Moscow.

АГГ҃Е ПРЕСТАТЕСНЕБЕСЕПСЛАНБЫ

The Annunciation. Fresco by
Dionisy, 1502-1503 (copy)

St. Apostle Andrew the First Called. Icon. 16th century (a fragment)

Baptism of Prince Vladimir. Frenco by Victor Vasnetsov in the Cathedral of St. Vladimir in Kiev. 19th century

"Kievan Prince Vladimir became inspired by the thought of becoming a Christian. He entered the Holy Font and was reborn by the Spirit and water; he was baptised in Christ and was saved" (Reverend Nestor. *Tale of Bygone Years*).

Celebrations of the one-thousandth anniversary of the Baptism of Russ at the monument to St. Prince Vladimir. It was precisely on that spot that St. Andrew the First Called prophesied: „Look at these hills. The Divine Grace will shine here and a great city will be erected, and God will create numerous churches."

"Many people gathered: they entered
the water some of them up to the neck,
others up to the breast holding children in
their arms. The priests were nearby praying. Vladimir lifted his eyes to their arms.
The priests were nearby praying. Vladimir
lifted his eyes to the sky and said: 'You
who created the sky and the earth! Accept
these new people" (St. Nestor. *Tale of
Bygone Years*).

"For us the Holy Virgin is Heaven.
She is the Divine Throne. In her God clad
Himself in a chasuble to save us" (St.
Efrem of Syria).

The St. Vladimir Cathedral in
Kiev. Architects I. Shtrom, P.
Sparro and A. Beretti. 1862-1882

Sts. Cyril and Methodius First Teachers of the Slavs. Icon of the 19th century

Thanks to Cyril and Methodius who had improved the Slavic alphabet, the Russians were able to use their native tongue in the church service immediately after baptism.

St. Princess Olga. Fresco of the 17th century

Olga "was a precursor in the Christian land like dawn that comes before the sun (Vladimir)... She was the first to enter the Kingdom of Heaven from Russia" (St. Nestor. Tale of Bygone Years).

The Golden Gate in Kiev. 1037. Restored in 1983

St. Princess Olga's stone tomb. 10th century.

Yaroslav the Wise "created the great and saintly house of God. This Church earned veneration and glory among the neighbouring people" (St. Illarion).

Sts. Boris and Gleb Icon, 12th century

Boris and Gleb, the first Russian saints, were called martyrs. They were the first in Russia to imitate the feat of the Redeemer. They meekly and voluntarily accepted their martyrdom from the hands of their brother.

The thirteen dome St. Sophia Cathedral in Kiev. 11th century

The Kiev-Pechery Lavra. Founded in 1051

"Some monasteries were built with gold and silver. The monastery of Feodosy (Pechersky) was built with his tears and prayers" (Life of St. Feodosy).

Nestor the chronicler described Alipy as a "skillful painter"

The shrine with the relics of St. Alipy—the icon painter who died in 1114

The great tree of the Kievan monasticism was raised by the labours and cares of two great elders from the Pechery Monastery — Antony and Feodosy — and florished with the God-pleasing deeds of its saints

The tree of the saints of the Pechery Monastery. Icon. 18th century

Just as Divine Transfiguration took place during a prayer on the Mount of Tabor, inner enlightenment and transfuguration takes place in every believer during his spiritual ascension.

The Pskov-Pechery Monastery of the Dormition. Founded in the 15th century

"Monasteries on the hills and monks" appeared all over Russia. Monasteries became the true examples of the Christian faith and piety.

St. Nikita the Stylite. Icon. 16th century

Blessed Efrosinya of Suzdal. Icon. 18th century

FROM THE DIVINE LITURGY OF SAINT JOHN CHRYSOSTOM
THE BEATITUDES:

In Thy Kingdom remember us,
O Lord: when Thou comest
into Thy Kingdom.
Blessed are the poor in spirit:
for theirs is the Kingdom
of Heaven.
Blessed are they that mourn:
for they shall be comforted.
Blessed are the meek:
for they shall inherit the earth.
Blessed are they that hunger
and thirst for righteousness:
for they shall be filled.
Blessed are the merciful:
for they shall obtain mercy.
Blessed are the pure in heart:
for they shall see God.
Blessed are the peacemakers:
for they shall be called
the sons of God.
Blessed are they
which are persecuted
for righteousness' sake:
for theirs is the Kingdom
of Heaven.
Blessed are ye,
when men shall revile you,
and persecute you,
and shall say all manner
of evil against you falsely,
for My sake.
Rejoice and be exceeding glad:
for great is your
reward in Heaven.

THE PRAYER
OF ST. EPHRAIM

Lord and Master of my life,
give me not a spirit of sloth,
vain curiosity,
lust for power, and idle talk.
But give to me Thy servant
a spirit of soberness,
humility, patience,
and love.
O Lord and King,
grant me to see my own faults
and not to condemn
my brother:
for blessed art Thou
to the ages of ages.
Amen.

The Dormition of the Most
Holy Mother of God, Icon by
Feofan the Greek. 1329

Many generations of monks lie buried
in the monastery's caves. The monks,
priests and laymen rever the memory of
these righteous men.

The Pskov-Pechery Monastery has always been the bulwark of the Orthodoxy in western Russia. Its main cathedral is dedicated to the Dormition of the Most Holy Mother of God.

УСПЕНІЕ ПРТЫА БЦЫ

52

Icon painting can be compared to "thinking in colours". The holy image depicted on an icon is mysteriously present in it. Therefore, the Orthodoxy regards icons as gracious shrine that can, through a prayer, produce a miraculous impact on man. To be able to bring to life the most perfect images of the invisible world on a piece of wood a painter should be pure in his spiritual vision.

Monk Zenon, an icon painter from the Pskov-Pechery Monastery

"God is the mystery of the world, life is the mystery of God". The Church contains in itself the eternal mystery of man's unity with the Creator. Being the depository of spiritual experience the Church is not only preserving our one-thousand-year long history but also discerns Divine Providence in it.

Dormition of the Most Holy Mother of God. Icon by monk Zenon

Archimandrite Ioann Krestyankin during a panikhida in the caves.

In addition to prayers and divine services every monk in the monasteries is entrusted with special duties with due account of his likings.

Convent of St. Trinity.
Founded in 1064.

Throughout its long history the Korets Convent in Volhynia have seen many disasters and been plundered more than once. Today, through the nuns' prayer and effort it is one of the best-run convents.

PRAYER TO THE GUARDIAN ANGEL

Holy Angel of Christ,
I fall down before thee
and pray to thee,
my holy guardian attached
to me to watch over my
soul and my sinful body
since Holy Baptism.
I have angered thy most
pure radiance and alienated
thee from myself by my
character and evil ways
and shameful deeds:
lies, calumnies, envy,
censure, haughtiness,
recalcitrance, brother-hatred,
unforgiveness, money-grubbing,
adultery, rancour, miserliness,
gluttony beyond satiety,
intemperate drinking,
garrulity, evil thoughts
and crafty designs,
bold manner and lewd debauchery,
and my craving for every
carnal pleasure.
Oh, my exectable lusts,
such as even the dumb animals
do not indulge!
How long canst thou
countenance me,
or approach me who stinks
like a dog?

With what eyes, Christ's Angel,
does thou perceive me,
caught as I am in evil
through my iniquities?
How can I ask for remission
of my vile and evil
and crafty deeds while
lapsing into these every
day and night and every hour?
Still I pray prostrating
myself before thee,
my holy guardian,
have mercy on me, a sinner,
thy unworthy servant (name),
help and protect me
in the face of my cruel
adversary with the holy prayers,
and enable me to partake
of God's Kingdom with all
the saints always,
today and ever and
in ages of ages.
Amen.

To become a monk or a nun is to abandon the earthly concerns for the heavenly concerns, to take the vows of celibacy, non-possession and obedience. Like the heavenly cities on the sinful earth they have shown a way to moral perfection and provided examples of love and tolerance. Today, festal services at monasteries attract numerous pilgrims.

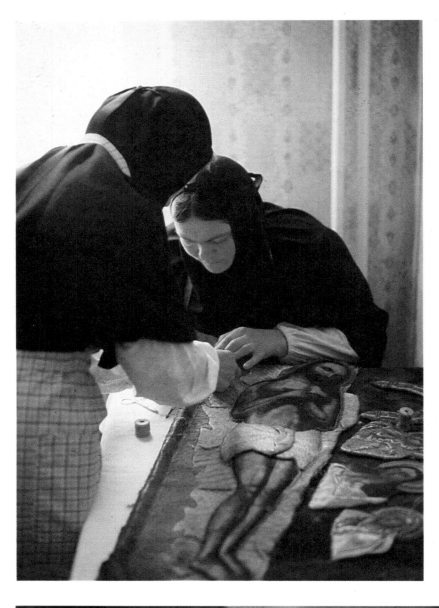

Protected by their heavenly patrons the nunneries in Korets and Pukhtitsa have survived through the most trying years in their history. Their icon lamps have never died out for a single day, neither did the prayers and righteous deed of the nuns and novices.

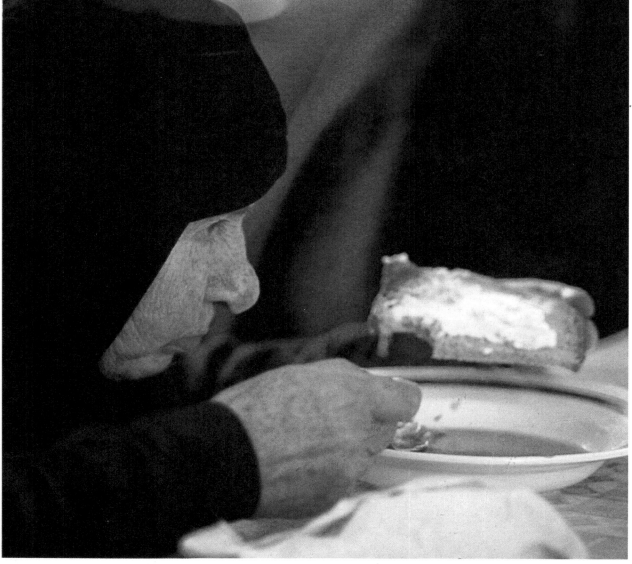

Blessed by the Mother Superior the nuns are diligently working on the monastery's lands, at the animal farm, the bee garden, the orchard and the greenhouse. Some of them are engaged in embroidery that they inherited from the times of the Kievan Rus.

Korets miracle working icon of the Mother of God

Today, the convents continue the old traditions and earn the gift of merciful love through constant prayer.

The Pükhtitsa Convent of the Dormition, founded in 1891

Natalia, Mother Superior of the
Korets Convent

65

The Mother of God Herself has pointed to Christian women the shortest, yet the most trying, way to salvation through self—denial and humility. Any pilgrim can find here respite and quiet joy.

"Be every work blessed." The nuns never start even a simple work without blesses and player."

"On the sixth day in the morning the pagans began their offensive on the town: some were carrying fire, others were pushing battering—rams. They seized Ryazan in December on the 21st day... They plundered the churches and killed many people at the holy altars. No one was left alive, everybody had equally to drink from the cup of death" (Lavrentievskaya Chronicle).

The Tartar-Mongol onslaught, an extract from *Life of Efrosinia of Suzdal*

The Cathedral of the Dormition of the Holy Mother of God in Vladimir.
12th century. See p. 70.

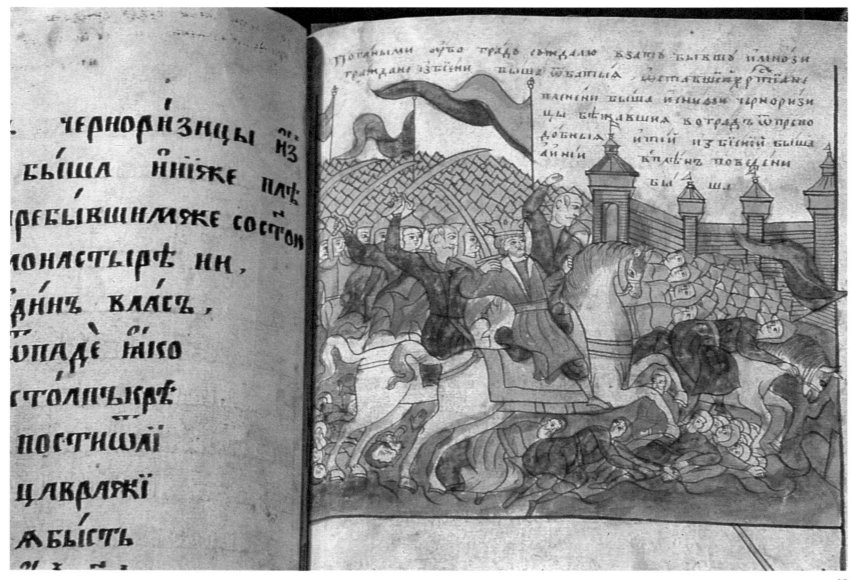

"...Our Lord brought pagans upon us for our many sins. Not because He wanted to make good into them, but to punish us so that we turn away from evil. Our Lord punished us with the pagans' onslaught" (Lavrentievskaya Chronicle).

Orthodox Grand Prince St. Aleksandr Nevsky. Icon from the Trinity Cathedral of the St. Aleksandr-Nevsky Lavra in Leningrad

Just like frost that locks in winter the earth and the rivers, the Horde shackled Russia. The Church alone remained the stronghold of faith and hope of salvation and unification for the sake of restoring the Russian statehood.

The Cathedral of the Transfiguration of the Saviour in Pereslavl-Zalesski. 1152-1154

Prince St. Daniil of Moscow. Fresco in the Archangel Cathedral in the Kremlin. 17th century

Prince Daniil was the founder of Moscovite Russia, he was "the first to lay the stone into the foundation of Moscow's present grandeur" so that "the memory of our ancestors would not fade and our candle continue burning".

In 1272 he set up the first monastery in Moscow dedicated to St. Daniel the Stylite, his heavenly patron. He died in it after taking vows of schema. The monastery was restored and reopened to mark the millennium of the baptism of Russia. Today, it is the spiritual centre of the Russian Orthodox Church.

One finds it hard to believe that the ruined monastery have for many years housed a colony for juvenile delinquents. The very thought that the children deprived of the knowledge of the Christian commandments and the Divine Word were living there causes pain.

St. Daniel Monastery see p. 76

The Cathedral of the Holy
Fathers of the Seven
Ecumenical Councils at the St.
Daniel Monastery

The St. Daniel Monastery was the
first out of twenty-three closed down and
plundered by the enemies of the Orthodoxy. In 1988, it was restored through the
prayer and effort of all righteous people
and with the help of the state at a high
cost. Nikolai Gogol, the great Russian
writer, was buried at the monastery's
graveyard, next to many rigteous man
from the monastery.

St. Trinity Cathedral of the
St. Daniel Monastery in
Moscow

PRAYER
TO THE ALL-HOLY
BIRTH-GIVER OF GOD

O All-Holy Sovereign Lady,
the Birth-giver of God,
Thou art above all angels
and archangels,
and more honourable,
than all creatures,
Hope of hopeless, Protector
of the poor, Comfort
of the sorrowing, Provider
to those that hunger, Clothing
to the naked, Healer to the sick,
Salvation to sinners,—
to all Christians Thou art
a Help and Protection.
O All-compassionate
Sovereign Lady, the Virgin
Birth-giver, by Thy benevolence
save and have mercy
upon the Right
Reverend Metropolitans,
Archbishops, Bishops,
all the clergy and monastic orders;
the governing bodies,
leaders of the armed
forces, all those in authority
and all Orthodox Christians
protect with Thy esteemed
mantle, and implore Him Who
became incarnate from Thee
without seed, Christ our God,

that he girdle us with power
from on high against our
visible and invisible foes.
O Most-benevolent Sovereign Lady,
elevate us from the depths
of sinfulness, and save
us from famine, destruction,
from earthquakes and drowning,
from fire and sword,
from hostile besiegement
and civil wars,
from sudden death and from
attacks by enemies,
and from all evil.
O Lady Most Pure, grant
peace and health to Thy servants,
all the Orthodox Christians,
enlighten their mind
and direct their spiritual
vision towards salvation;
vouchsafe unto us,
Thy sinful servants,
the Kingdom of Thy Son,
Christ our God.
For His sovereignty
is blessed and all-glorious,
with His unoriginate Father,
and with the All-Holy and Good
and Life-giving Spirit,
now and ever, and unto ages
of ages. Amen.

St. Petr, Metropolitan
of Moscow and All Russia,
Miracle-Worker.
Icon by Dionisy,
15th century.

St. Petr, Metropolitan
of Moscow and All Russia,
Miracle-Worker.
Icon by Dionisy,
15th century.

In his last hour Metropolitan Petr gave his blessing to erecting a Cathedral of the Dormition of the Mother of God in the Kremlin, seeing it as a future main church of Holy Russia.

The Cathedral of the
Dormition in the Kremlin.
1475—79

Metropolitans of Moscow Petr and Aleksy, two grand figures of the Russian Orthodox Church, were sent to humiliated Russia during the Trying years of the Horde yoke to pray for their Motherland and perform the main tasks, that of the spiritual resurrection of the nation and uniting the Russian lands around Moscow.

84

Being the god-father of Prince Dimitry of Moscow, the hero of the Kulikovo battle, Metropolitan of Moscow Aleksy had for many years been carrying the burden of Church and state administration and multiplying the forces of Moscow Principality while the prince was a minor.

Interior of the Cathedral of the Dormition

The Nativity of the Blessed Virgin Mary. Icon, 15th century

The Cathedral of the Nativity of the Most Holy Mother of God built on the place where the Russian warriors, killed in the battle of Kulikovo, were buried.

The place where the river Nepryadva flows into the Don on the field of Kulikovo.

On September 8, 1380, on the Feast of the Nativity of the Most Holy Mother of God, a fierce battle between the Russians and the Horde forces took place on the field of Kulikovo. The Russian victory over the Tartar forces had a world historic significance. It marked the beginning of a mighty Russian state based around the Moscow Principality which proclaimed that "God is with the truth, not force".

Built on voluntary donations the monument to Prince Dimitry Donskoi on the Krasny Kholm marked the victory over Khan Mamai. 1850. Architect A. Brullov.

The Life-Giving Trinity. Icon
by St. Andrei Rublev.
1422—27

St. Sergy of Radonezh is everywhere revered as the Father Superior of the Russian Land. The founder of the monastery dedicated to the Holy Trinity he spent his life in the efforts to overcome "the disunity in the world". "His spiritual disciples were one of the chief spiritual forces that brought together the semi-pagan tribes scattered across Northern and Central Russia to form a united Great Russian nation fortified and tied together by the Orthodoxy".

(*From a sermon by Bichop Nikanor*).

Fragment of an embroidered portrait shroud of St. Sergy of Radonezh. Embroidery, about 1424

The Trinity-St. Sergy Lavra.
Founded in 1337

"I honour the saintly witnesses of the holiness of the fore-fathers in the splendid churches, I like your divine service but I want to see the wilderness... Who will show me the small wooden church that was the first to be dedicated to the Holy Trinity? Show me the entrance to the cell that St. Sergy built with his own hands in one day for which he was rewarded with a morsel of stale bread. Open the door of the tiny cell so that I can breathe the air still filled with the saint's prayers, it is washed with his tears and been an imprint of his prophetic words.

"All this is here. It is concealed with the time and restricted by these monumental buildings as a precious thing in a sumptuous box".

(From a sermon by Metropolitan Filaret (Drozdov)

PRAYER TO ST. SERGY, THE MIRACLE-WORKER OF RADONEZH
(September 25)

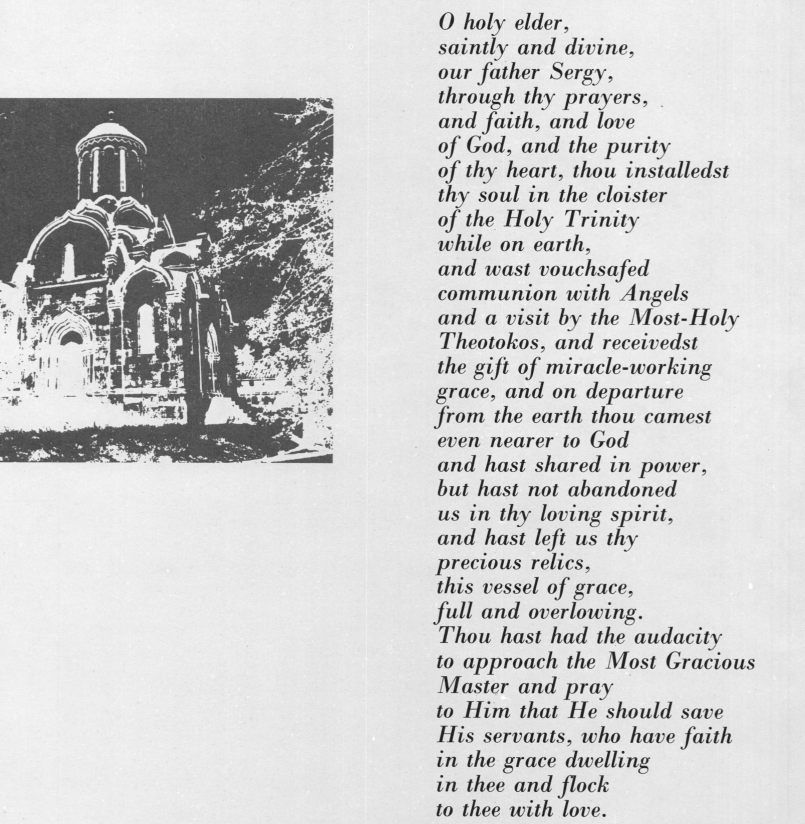

O holy elder,
saintly and divine,
our father Sergy,
through thy prayers,
and faith, and love
of God, and the purity
of thy heart, thou installedst
thy soul in the cloister
of the Holy Trinity
while on earth,
and wast vouchsafed
communion with Angels
and a visit by the Most-Holy
Theotokos, and receivedst
the gift of miracle-working
grace, and on departure
from the earth thou camest
even nearer to God
and hast shared in power,
but hast not abandoned
us in thy loving spirit,
and hast left us thy
precious relics,
this vessel of grace,
full and overlowing.
Thou hast had the audacity
to approach the Most Gracious
Master and pray
to Him that He should save
His servants, who have faith
in the grace dwelling
in thee and flock
to thee with love.
Pray that our All-Generous

God should grant us every
gift beneficial
to each and all:
purity in faith, deliverance
from hunger and affliction,
protection from the invasion
of aliens, consolation
to those in grief,
recovery to the ailing,
restoration to the virtue
to the fallen, return to the path
of truth and salvation
to the erring, fortitude
to ascetics, success
and blessing to those
engaged in good works,
upbringing to children,
edification to the young,
conversion to unbelievers,
good preparation
and encouragement to those
leaving this temporal
life for the life eternal,
and blessed repose
to the departed.
Deliver us through thy
interceding prayers
from torment on Doomsday,
so that we may find
ourselves among the righteous
and hear that blessed call
of Christ our Master:
«Come ye, those blessed
by My Father, and inherit
the Kingdom prepared for ye
since the creation
of the world.»
Amen.

St. Sergy of Radonezh.
Painting by M. Nesterov. 1899

"Rejoice, thou who wast
admitted to the Blessed
Heavenly Abode in thy
time...
Rejoice, thou who from
thy mother's womb
desiredst to be called
up for the service of
the Heavenly King like
a loyal soldier...
Rejoice, who thou hast
been vindicated by
God's grace... Rejoice,
thou precious, chosen
fruit of good parents...
Rejoice, thou
banisher of evil sorrows
in every undertaking...
Rejoice, o
Sergy, thou quick helper
and most glorious mi-
racle-worker."

*(From the Akathistos
to St. Sergy of Radonezh)*

A thanksgiving service on
St. Sergy's memorial day

Monument to St. Sergy by
V. Klykov. 1988

Great Martyr St. George the
Victorious. Icon. 15th century
(see overleaf)

Dome of the Ivan the Great
belfry in the Kremlin built
in 1600 under Tzar Boris
Godunov (see overleaf)

Having lived through many trials Orthodox Russia emerged purified and enlightened, she was aware of her power and righteousness and was ready to follow along the road charted for her people by Divine Providence towards peace and salvation in the Church.

Moscow Kremlin Cathedrals

Monastery of the Nativity in
Borovsk founded by St.
Pafnuty in 1444

St. Kirill of the Beloe Lake
shown on the silver lid of
a shrine (The Armoury)

St. Sergy blessed his pupils and disciples to go to distant lands, settle in along rivers and lakes, set up chapels and cloisters in thick woods. Through their efforts the candle of the Orthodoxy first lit at the Life-Giving Trinity cloister of Father Surerior Sergy was brought to new places.

The Savvino-Storozhevsky Monastery of the Nativity, founded in 1398

St. Iosif of Volokolamsk. Icon.
17th century

Iosif of Volokolamsk, the great zealot, was active in the Volokolamsk land where he founded a monastery with extremely strict rules. He was a skillful worker. His behests and teaching retain their spiritual significance to this day.

A builder of churches, the man who inspired the icon painter and an enlightener Dionisy, Iosif was buried in his monastery in the Cathedral of the Dormition.

The Dormition Monastery of St. Iosif of Volokolamsk. Founded in 1479.

Metropolitan Pitirim of
Volokolamsk and Yuriev,
Head of the Publishing
Department of the Moscow
Patriarchate, during
a service

The Novodevichy Convent in
Moscow. Founded in 1542 (see p. 106)

The icon shows St. Vasily the Blessed as he is preserved in the memory of the nation. A strange creature he went about naked in summer and in winter. He meekly accepted blows, derision, reverence and pity. He entered the difficult path of a "God's fool" by the Divine command when he was sixteen. He could forecast natural calamities and changes of fortune and was aware of people's thoughts. He was shedding tears for man's sinful nature and was praying for those who lost the true path in life. He was buried under the Cathedral of the Protection of the Virgin.

The Cathedral of the Holy Trinity, or of the Protection of the Virgin, commonly known as the Cathedral of St. Vasily the Blessed. It was built to mark the capture of Kazan by Ivan the Terrible in 1555.

Tzar Ivan the Terrible. 18th century

Novodevichy Convent (see overleaf)

This cathedral is crowned with many domes: there is a Moorish, an Indian, a Byzantine and a Chinese dome, united by a Russian cupola rising above them.

"This is not for us but in Your name and glory' our ancestors were saying while setting up the crosses on the varied domes of the St. Vasily the Blessed Cathedral. The idea of this splendid building is totally clear: it is the task of Russia to unite all peoples and show them the way to heaven".

(*Patriarch Sergy Stragorodsky*)

Ivan the Terrible goes on a pilgrimage. Painting by N. Sverchkov. 19th century

Exaltation of the Cross. Icon.
15th century

Ivan the Terrible was one of the best educated men of his time. A quick-minded polemicist, he was also a good stylist and composer. The Russian state was his main concern: he was striving to return those parts that had been taken away from it by enemies. He did a lot of good but fell victim to his natural pride.Combined with absolute power he weilded in Russia it brought disaster to the royal family. God resisteth the proud.

Metropolitan Philipp was bold enough to oppose the tzar and his highhanded pen and violence. He defended the tzar's innocent victims. Ivan the Terrible defrocked him on his own will and the Metropolitan died the death of a martyr.

Tzar Ivan the Terrible and Metropolitan Philipp in the Cathedral of the Dormition. Painting of the 19th century

St. Philipp, Metropolitan of Moscow and All Russia, a miracle-worker. Icon. 17th century

Iov, a portrait from a book of the 17th century

Shortly before the Time of Troubles settled in the Eastern Patriarchs agreed that Moscow establish a patriarchate of its own. Iov, Father Superior of the Staritsa Monastery, was elected the first Patriarch of Moscow and All Russia. In the Time of Troubles Patriachs remained the only stronghold of the state that was perishing without a head.

"The Mother of God, save the Orthodoxy", was Patriarch Iov's reply to those who came to him to demand that he would crown the False Dimitry. He flatly rejected any attempts to persuade him: "Here I witness great troubles for the country and the triumph of deceit and heresy". The faithful believers seemed to be completely misguided. While before they used to say: "We love our country as a mother loves her infant", at the Time of Troubles many were prepared to sacrifice the infant.

Staritsa Monastery of the Dormition. Founded in 1110

The Slain Prince Dimitry. Painting by M. Nesterov. 1899

The murder of Prince Dimitry who was eight years old and the lies that were piled up around his name were redeemed by rivers of Christian blood.

The Cathedral in Uglich built on the place where Prince Dimitry was stabbed to death. 1692

Prince Volkonsky's death at the shrine of St. Pafnuty of Borovsk. Painting. 19th century

Peasants Shilov and Slotov blow up the Polish underground passage. Lithograph. 19th century

Don Icon of the Mother of God.
Icon. 1380

Prince Dimitry's relics are
moved from Uglich to Moscow.
Icon. 18th century

Patriarch Iov refuses to recognise the False Dimitry. Painting by P. Geller. 19th century

The removal of the relics of the saint infant to Moscow failed to convince the people: unruly crowds continued to listen to the evil rumours that the Prince had been saved and needed help to regain the parental throne.

Prince Dimitry's image on the lid of the shrine. Gilded silver. 17th century

Martyr St. Germogen,
Patriarch of Moscow and All
Russia. Icon. 19th century

Imprisoned in the Monastery of St. Michael's Miracle, Patriarch Germogen called on the entire nation to be ready to die for the Orthodox faith. This was his last address to the Orthodox believers.

Patriarch Germogen's Charter.
Original of the 17th century

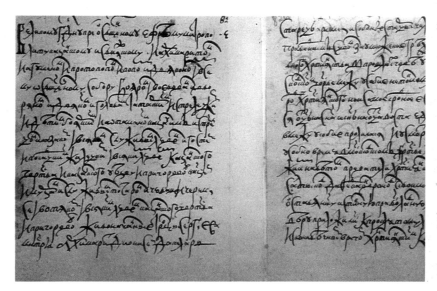

Monastery of St. Michael's Miracle in Chonae in the Kremlin. Founded in 1366

Nizhni Novgorod. Painting by
G. Chernetsov. 19th century

Russia will always
remember the feat
of Nizhni Novgorod
that rose like one
man to follow Kozma
Minin Sukhoruk to
liberate their
Motherland from
the Poles.

The Transfiguration of the
Saviour Monastery in
Yaroslavl from where Duke
Dimitry Pozharsky and his
army began their offensive on
Moscow

Monument to citizen Minin and
Duke Pozharsky by I. Martos.
1818

The Heavenly Church gives divine
power to the earthly Church through the
miracle working icons and the relics of
saints. This is a great mystery.

St. Prince Dimitry. Icon. 18th
century

The Kazan Icon of the Mother of God became the symbol of the liberation of Moscow from the occupants and rebels.

123

PRAYER TO OUR LORD JESUS CHRIST

*All-Wise and All-Merciful Lord,
our Saviour!
Thou, Who Enlightened with the
radiance of Thy coming the four
corners of the world and summoned
us to Thy Holy Church
with the promise of goods
incorruptible and everlasting,
behold us, Thy unworthy
servants, graciously,
and do not remember our
trespasses but forgive us all
our sins in Thy infinite mercy.
Even though we violate
Thy Holy Will, we do not
renounce Thee, our God
and Saviour: we sin against
Thee Alone, but also
serve Thee Alone,
believe in Thee Alone,
have recourse to Thee Alone
and want to be Thy
servants only.
Remember the weakness
of our nature and the temptations
the adversary holds out
to us everywhere,
and the charms and seductions
of the world, in the face
of which, as it is said,
we are helpless but for Thee.*

Cleanse us and save us Thyself!
Enlighten our minds Thyself,
so that we may steadfastly
make our hearts love Thee Alone,
our only God and Creator.
Direct our steps Thyself,
so that we may proceed
unstumblingly in the light
of Thy commandments.
Truly, our Lord and Saviour,
show us Thy great
and beneficent mercy:
see to it that we may
spend every day of our life
in sanctity and truth
and thus deserve, at Thy
glorious second coming,
to hear Thy gracious call
to the Kingdom of Heaven,
vouchsafe that we,
Thy sinful and unworthy
servants, are received into
it and are enabled,
in enjoying its unspeakable
beauty, to glorify Thee
with Thy Father,
Who is without beginning,
and with the Eternal
Divine Spirit in ages of ages.
Amen.

Domes of the chamber churches.
1684 (see overleaf)

St. Nicholas the Miracle-
Worker. Icon. 15th century

128

Moscow, and the entire Russian land is standing thanks to the prayers of the chosen saints. Tired of bloodshed and lawlessness it was craving for peace and a blessing for creation.

The harvest. Life of Prophet Elisha. Fresco. 1680-81

The tree of the Muscovite State. Icon by Simon Ushakov. 17th century

The tzar and the Patriarch, the heads of temporal and spiritual power, are tending together the thriving tree of the Muscovite State for they know that the Almighty blesses a united state and the Church and helps people to prosper and multiple.

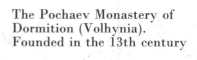

The Orthodox believers whom the Uniates persecuted for their faith came to St. Iov into cave to seek consolation and protection. The Monastery in Pochaev belonged to the Uniates for 110 years.

Subjugated by the Catholic Poland and Lithuania the Russian lands of Small Russia and Belaya Russia united with Moscow in 1654 and returned to their spiritual mother, the Russian Orthodox Church.

The shrine of St. Iov of Pochaev

Cathedral of the
Transfiguration of the Saviour
in Zvenigorod. 13th century

Since time immemorial our land was beautified with churches, monasteries, palaces and towers and walls of kremlins in Russian cities and towns. Many champions of the Orthodoxy worked to multiply the monumental buildings. People gladly contributed to the creative work blessed and bequeathed by the Maker.

The Kremlin in Rostov the Great. 17th century

133

Tzar Alexei Mikhailovich. 17th
century

Having admitted two fraternal
Orthodox nations into his state the tzar
regarded himself as the head of a mighty
power.

Tzar Alexei Mikhailovich
reviews the army at the
Novodevichy Convent.
Painting by N. Sverchkov. The
Armoury

New Jerusalem, a monastery
on the Istra. Founded in 1656

Patriarch Nikon who was also a gifted architect and a profound thinker in quest for hidden knowledge, was aware of the great role the Orthodoxy had to play in the destiny of mankind. He built New Jerusalem on the Istra near Moscow in imitation of the heavenly Jerusalem.

Patriarch Nikon and the
prayerful. Portrait. 18th
century

According to the 1649 Code of Laws
the Monastery Department began interfering little by little into the affairs of the
Church and tried to keep the Church
down. An agreement between the Tzar and
the Church came to an end.

Sobornoe ulozhenie, the Code of
Laws of 1649

Revised prayer-book. 17th century

After Patriarch Nikon and the Tzar severed their relations, Nikon was stripped of the holy orders at the Council attended by the Eastern Patriarchs. This was a tragic hour for our Church. Revision of prayer-books, symbols and rites resulted in a schism.

Nikon is deprived of patriarchal dignity at the Local Council. Painting. 19th century

The Holy Virgin "The Burning
Bush". Icon. 17th century

"O Christ, our God, Who in the shape of a bush burning with fire and yet not burning showedst Moses Thy Most Pure Mother Who had received the fire of the Divinity in her womb and was not burnt and stayed unimpaired even upon giving birth, rid us, through Her prayers, of the flames of passions and keep Thy city from fire and arson, for Thou art Greatly Merciful".

(Troparion to the Icon of the Mother of God "The Burning Bush")

Those who suspected Patriarch Nikon and his followers of a bias towards Catholicism regarded it honourable to die for their faith.

Old Believers burn themselves.
Drawing by G. Myasoedov.
19th century

Peter the Great deprived the Russian Orthodox Church of the Patriarchal guidance and transferred it under the guidance of the Chief—Procurator and the Synod.

At that stage an encounter with the Western world — view bred atheism in the upper circles and disdain for the Russian values. Later, numerous intellectuals would look for ideals in alien lands.

St. Dimitry of Rostov. Portrait
by V. Borovikovsky. 18th
century

At the same time, the Church was granted with the shining examples of faith and dedication: Tikhon Zadonsky, Mitrofan of Voronezh, Dimitry of Rostov...

St. Dimitry of Rostov. Portrait
by V. Borovikovsky. 18th
century

Rostov the Great. Founded in
the 9th century

A procession at the St. Nil Hermitage. Lithography. 19th century

"The saints live in a different world where they perceive the glory of God by the Holy Spirit. They perceive our life and our deeds through the same Holy Spirit." (Starets Siluan)

St. Nil of Stolobnoye. Wooden sculpture. 19th century

St. Nil Hermitage today

St. Paisy Velichkovsky.
Portrait of the 18th century

"It is difficult to describe the holy zealots' inner life. God alone is aware of their feats, their deeds, temptations and inner struggle that can be intense at time and that is crowned with an inner victory".

(Vasily Klyuchevsky, Old Russian Lives of Saints)

A Moldavian Father Superior Paisy resurrected the old tradition of spiritual councelling

Multi—image icon.

St. Serafim of Sarov

"The meaning of life lies in the attempt to acquire the Holy Divine Spirit, the 'breathing of life' that placed man above all the creatures and likens him to God" (St. Serafim of Sarov)

PRAYER OF THE OPTINA HERMITAGE SAINTLY ELDERS

O Lord,
grant that I may face
everything this day
holds in store for me
with equanimity.
O Lord,
grant that I may wholly
resign myself on Thy Will.
O Lord,
instruct and support me
every hour of this day.
O Lord,
reveal Thy Will to me
and those around me.
Whatever tidings I receive
in the course of the day,
grant that I may
receive them with peace
in my soul and the firm
conviction that everything
happens according
to Thy Will.
O Lord,
Great and Gracious,
guide my thoughts
and feelings in all
my deeds and words;
in all unforeseen circumstances,
do not let me forget
that everything is
decreed by Thee.
O Lord,
grant that I may deal
prudently with everyone

near and dear to me,
offending none and
embarassing none.
O Lord,
give me the strength
to endure the weariness
of this day
and all its events.
Guide my will and teach
me to pray and love
everyone without
partiality.
Amen.

Hieroschemamonk Lev
Hieroschemamonk Makary
Saint Amvrosy
Hieroschemamonk Ilarion
Hieroschemamonk Iosif
Hieroschemamonk Anatoly
Schemaarchimandrite Var-
sonofy
Hieroschemamonk Anatoly
H i e r o s c h e m a m o n k
Anatoly, Jr.
Hieroschemamonk Nektary
Hieromonk Nikon
Schemamonk Makary Opta
Hegumen Avraamy
Schemaarchimandrite Moisey
Schemahegumen Antony
Schemaarchimandrite Ksenofont
Schemaarchimandrite Isaaky
Schemahegumen Feodosy
Schemaarchimandrite Sevastian
Schemaarchimandrite
Isaaky the Second
Hegumen Ioann

The Monastery of the
Presentation of the Blessed
Virgin (Optina Hermitage).
Founded in the 14th century

Hieroschemamonk Lev.
Engraving

"Nowhere have I seen such monks.
I did not ask them how they were living:
everything could be seen on their faces".

(Nikolai Gogol)

The starets St. Amvrosy.
Photo. 19th century

Hieroschemamonk Makary.
Engraving

The Cathedral of St. John the Baptist in the Optina Hermitage

News about the kind starets Amvrosy spread across Russia. Thousands found salvation in him.

The pilgrims' house in the Optina Hermitage

Pilgrims from all corners of Russia came to the Optina Hermitage on the day of memory of the venerable starets to attend the feast procession and the moleben held after many decades of abomination of desolation.

Long before Amvrosy was canonized people set up a grave stone on the place where he had been buried on the desecrated cemetery

The Day of Judgement. Icon. 17th century

Metropolitan of Moscow Filaret (Drozdov). Portrait. 19th century

The 19th century came down in the history of the Russian Church as the age of Filaret. He was a prominent theologian and a highly educated person. At the same time he was a genuine ascetic monk. His eloquent and profound sermons, many of which were translated into foreign languages, earned him the name of Moscow Chrysostom. He did translations from Greek and Hebrew into Russian and wrote poetry. He was the author of the famous Manifesto of February 19, 1861, that liberated the peasants of Russia.

The Trinity—St. Sergy Lavra

Russia at the Cross. Painting
by M. Nesterov

In the contradictory 19th century good seed and tares were sown in Russia. The Orthodox faith alone could protect popular consciousness from temptation and seduction fraught with tragedies.

It seems that the 20th century threw open the gates of hell, and hatred and rage flooded Russia. The Russian Orthodox Church became a Martyr Church. It has lived through the trials the Christendom never saw.

The Cathedral of Christ the Saviour. Architect K. Ton

St. Tikhon. Patriarch of
Moscow and All Russia. Photo

Tzar Nicholas II. Potrait.
19th century

In 1918, the entire royal family died the deaths of martyrs.

God and the Divine commandments have long been rejected in Russia in defiance of all ethical and moral norms.

Archpriest St. Ioann of Kronstadt. Photo. 19th century

Hundreds of thousands of clerics and millions of believers perished at that time. Hundreds of monasteries and tens of thousands of churches were destroyed.

Patriarch Tikhon had to shoulder the burden of the suffering Church in the time of trials.

PRAYER OF THE RUSSIAN ORTHODOX CHURCH ABROAD FOR THE SALVATION OF RUSSIA

*Lord Jesus Christ, our God,
receive this fervent
prayer from us,
Thy unworthy servants,
and, forgiving us all
our transgressions,
remember all our
adversaries, who hate
and offend us.
Do not visit their
deeds upon them but,
in Thy great mercy,
convert them — make
the unfaithful embrace
Orthodoxy and piety,
and the faithful turn
away from evil and do good.
And, through Thy infinite
power, graciously
deliver us all,
and Thy Holy Church,
from every evil affliction.
Free our Home Country
of the fierce atheists
and their sway;
hearken, our gracious God,
to the pained wail*

of Thy faithful servants
crying to Thee in grief
and sorrow day and night,
and raise their lives
from decay.
Give peace and calm,
love and dignity
and an early reconciliation
to Thy people, whom Thou
hast redeemed with Thy
precious Blood.
But be also revealed
to those who have
renounced Thee and
do not seek Thee,
so that not a single
one of them may perish
but that all of them may
be saved and see
the truth, and that all
of them may, in harmony
of thought and infinite
love, glorify Thy
virtuous name,
O Long-Suffering,
Mild Lord, in ages of ages.
Amen.

MARTYRS
OF THE 20TH CENTURY

Archbishop Ilarion Troitsky

Father Pavel Florensky

"Since the earthly and visible Church forms only a part of the entire Church it acts and supervises within its limits without condemning the rest of mankind. It recognises as excommunicated only those who cut off from it by their own free will.

"It speaks for the rest of mankind at the Day of Judgement. The earthly Church judges itself by the Spirit and Freedom given to it through Christ. It calls on all to unite and become sons of God through Christ" (A. Khomyakov).

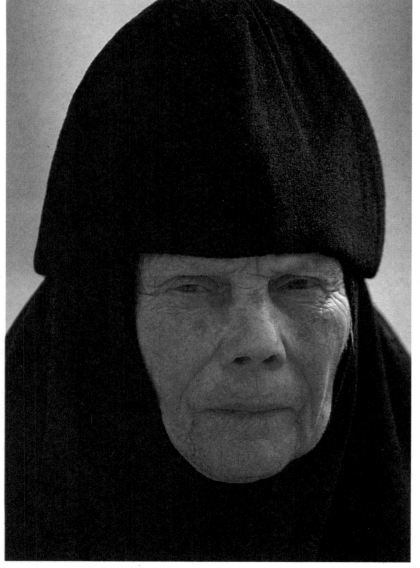

ВОЗДВИЖЕНІЄ ЧЕСТ ИꙖГО КРЕСТА ГДНꙖ

Installation of the Cross. Icon
by monk Zenon

The Meeting of the Vladimir
Icon of the Mother of God.
Icon.

"When the heart is full of repentance and self-condemnation a short and sincere prayer can express these feelings" (St. Ignaty Bryanchaninov).

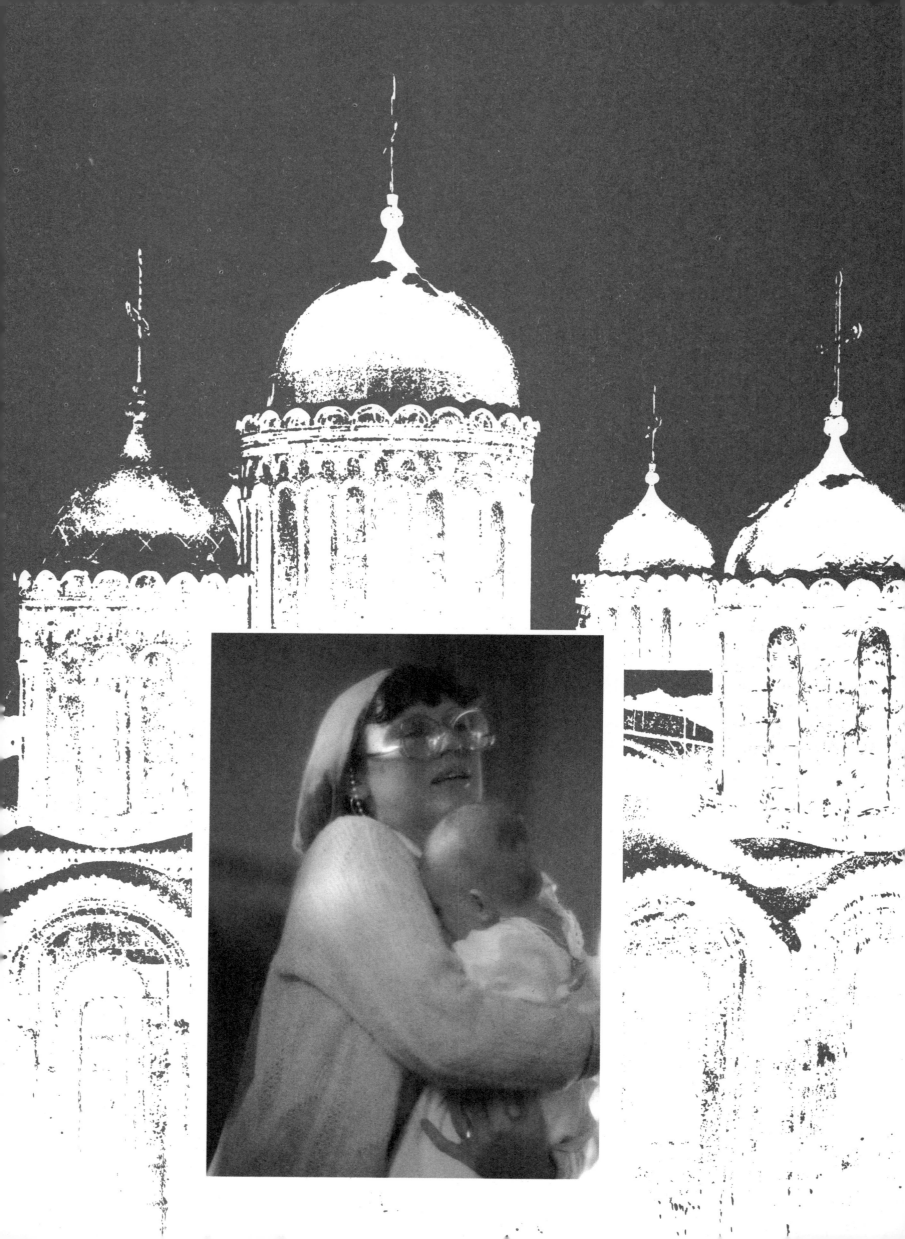

An altar and other ecclesiastical requisites made by workers of the Sofrino workshops.

The Church gives its blessing to the marital union of a bride and a groom through the Sacrament of Matrimony that imitates the spiritual union of Christ and the Church and asks their union to be blessed with children and their maturity in Christ.

Mitre, liturgical headdress worn by hierarchs

Artophorion

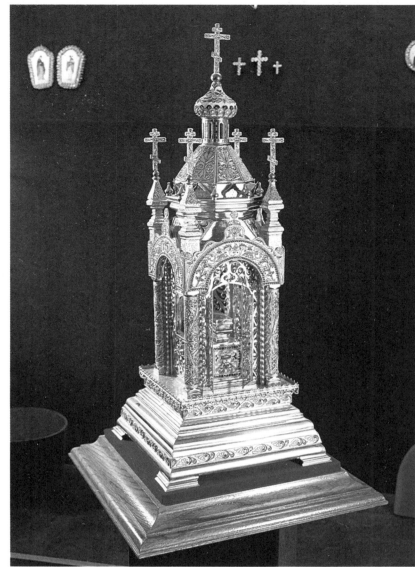

Consecration of a bishop

Alexy, Metropolitan of Leningrad and Novgorod

The Church selects the most worthy from among its children to perform the salutary sacraments through the rites of consecration that continue uninterrupted from the times of the Apostles.

Chalice

Gedeon, Metropolitan
of Stavropol and Baku

"My soul, my soul, arise! Why are you sleeping? The end is drawing near, and you will be confounded. Awake, then, and be watchful, that Christ, our God may spare you, Who is everywhere present and fills all things".

(The kontakion of the Great Canon of St. Andrew of Crete)

"There are seven gifts of the Holy Spirit," says Isaiah. There are also seven sacraments performed by the Holy Spirit. They are: Baptism, Chrismation, Eucharist, Confession, Holy Orders, Matrimony and Extreme Unction."

(Simeon, Archbishop of Thessalonika)

When giving Communion to a baby the priest says: «The servant of God (name) partakes of the precious and holy Body and Blood of our Lord and God and Savior Jesus Christ unto life eternal.»

The Church teaches that our life does not end when our earthly way is over.

Pitirim, Metropolitan of Volokolamsk and Yuriev, Professor of the Moscow Theological Academy and his students. The Trinity — St.Sergy Lavra.

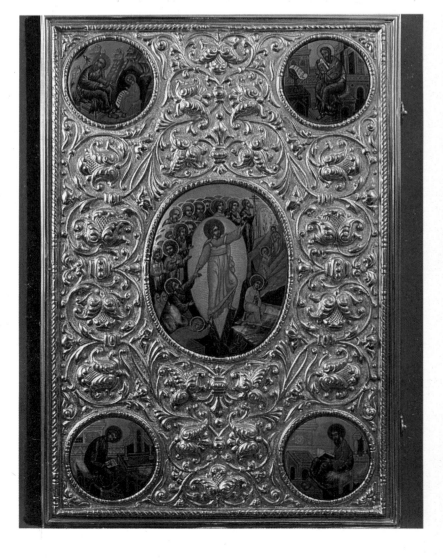

"It is the main task of our theological schools to train the priests and theologians worthy of their titles and ready to work for the glory of Christ"

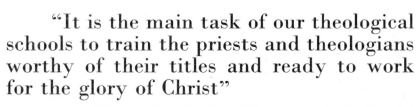

(*Pimen, Patriarch of Moscow and All Russia*)

Contemporary altar Gospel

Contemporary panagia and pectoral cross

During the eight years that they spend in the seminary and the academy the future priests study the Holy Scripture, theology, church history, liturgy, the old and new languages, church singing, the history of their Motherland.

PRAYER TO COMMEMORATE THE MILLENNIUM OF RUSSIA'S CHRISTIANIZATION

*O Trinitarian God Almighty,
Only-Begotten Son, Saviour
of the world and Holy Spirit,
Thou enlightenest
and sanctifiest peoples
and nations, Thou hast also
converted Prince Vladimir,
the sovereign of the Land
of Russ, to the light
of the true faith and thus
enlightened the whole
of our country through
Baptism and granted us
a dazzling host of saints,
who adorn the heaven
of the Russian Church
like radiant stars!
Thou hast also granted us,
Thy humble and unworthy
children, who are facing
Thy glory today and chanting
prayers of gratitude
on this millennial day
of the Baptism of Russ,
the great joy of glorifying,
praising and thanking
Thee for all the favours
Thou hast bestowed on Russia
since ancient times to this day.
Behold thy field,
the Holy Church, and our home
land, which donate Thee saints,
the splendid fruit of the salvific
sowing of Thy Word.*

*They have served people
with their faith, hope and love,
they have shown us the path to
perfection with their word and living,
according to Christ's promise:
ye shall be as perfect
as your Heavenly Father is.
We preserve their holy heritage
and pray to Thee, the Life-Giver:
save us and have mercy on us, give
peace to Thy world
and to all Thy creation,
seing that through our sins
the sons of this century
live in fear of death. For we know
that Thou dost not desire
the sinners' death, but desirest them
to be converted and live! Behold us,
bestow repentance on us and spare
us in Thy unspeakable mercy.
Receive our prayers and labours
aimed at enhancing
love among the people of this world.
Protect the Land of Russia,
give wisdom to the powers
that be, comfort and gladden everyone,
make Thy Church grow, preserve Thy
possessions, enlighten male, and
female, and child with Thy grace,
and strengthen all Thy people
in Orthodoxy and piety through
the prayers of Thy Most
Pure Mother and the power
of the Precious Life-Giving
Cross and all the saints
who have shone in this country,
so that we may, in unity
of faith and love, glorify Thee,
Father and Son and Holy Spirit,
in ages of ages.
Amen.*

Pimen, Patriarch of Moscow and All Russia

The general service at the Cathedral of Epiphany opened celebrations of the one-thousandth anniversary of the baptism of Russia.

Praying were Their Holinesses and Beatitudes Primates and representatives of the Local Orthodox Churches and religious associations participants in the Local Council of the Russian Orthodox Church.

Patriarch Teoctist of Rumania, and Patriarch Diodoros of Jerusalem during the service

During the jubilee, the old church objects of worship, that had been confiscated, were returned to the Russian Orthodox Church at the Armoury.

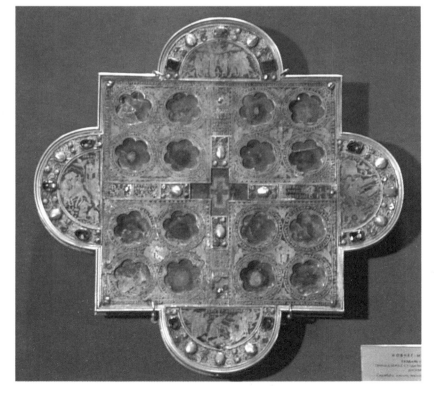

Pyx with relics

On June 6, 1988, the Local Council of the Russian Orthodox Church was opened in the Refectory Church of St. Sergy of Radonezh in the Trinity-St. Sergy Lavra. It lasted for four days (see overleaf).

The Kremlin cathedrals. 1988

A historic meeting between Mikhail Gorbachev and Partiarch Pimen and permanent members of the Holy Synod of the Russian Orthodox Church took place on April 29, 1988. They discussed some of the concrete questions related to church life and activity.

The life of faith was not extinguished in the Russian land under the protection of the Most Holy Mother of God and in answer to the prayers of Russian saints and all the martyrs and righteous men. The Church entered the year of the one-thousandth anniversary of the baptism of Russia with an awareness that it has fulfilled its historic mission of salvation.

The main events at the Local Council were: canonisation of new saints and adoption of a New Statute of the Russian Orthodox Church.

On June 12 a solemn divine service was conducted in the St. Daniel Monastery in Moscow. It was attended by thousands of worshippers. On that memorable day the Patriarch said: "Today we are aware of the Protection Veil of the Mother of God which as an invisible cover is spread over the entire multimillion Russian congregation given to us by God. We are aware of the spiritual affinity all the saints and righteous men in the Russian land from Boris and Gleb who were the first to be canonised in Russia to the recently canonised saints Makary, Ignaty, Feofan, Andrei, Maksim, Paisy and Amvrosy, Prince Dimitry and the Blessed Ksenia."

"The first ten centuries of our Church are coming to an end. God help us to enter in peace and piety into the next millennium of our existence in the House of God which is the Church of the Living God, the pillar and ground of the truth."

"As a beautiful fruit of Thy salvific
sowing the land of Russia offers Thee,
O Lord, all the saints that have shone in it.
By their prayers preserve the Church and
our land in deep peace through the
Theotokos, O Greatly-Merciful One".

*(Troparion to the saints
of the Land of Russia, Tone 8)*

Iliya II, Catholicos-Patriarch
of All Georgia

"Let us flock to the Protectress of our land, the Ever-Virgin Theotokos, and worship Her first-painted icon, crying out from the depth of our heart: O Mother of God, save the Land of Russia, heal her wounds and console the faithful".

(Same troparion, tone 4)

In Moscow, Kiev, Vladimir, Leningrad, Minsk and other cities where the one-thousandth anniversary of the baptism of Russia was celebrated the worshippers paid tribute to their compatriots who died in the Great Patriotic War of 1941-1945. Their number was tremendous. May their memory live for ever!

While watching the solemn procession one feels that the entire history of Russia was the Road to Calvary our nation travelled along together with its Redeemer. The Orthodox believers were subjected to numerous temptations in the 1000 years that have passed. Every time departed from the truth they had to pay with strife, internecine wars and other tragic events.

Every time the Holy Spirit gave the Orthodox people enough strenght to repent and realise their delusions. Every time they returned to the love of God, Jesus Christ.

Filaret, Metropolitan of Minsk and Grodno, Patriarchal Exarch to Byelorussia, is blessing the believers.

Patriarch Pimen stood at the head of the Church when it was living through another historic event in its history: 400 years of the Patriarchate in Russia. His predecessors were:

Iov (1589-1605)
Germogen (1606-1612)
Filaret (1619-1633)
Ioasaf I (1634-1641)
Iosif (1642-1652)
Nikon (1652-1658)
Ioasaf II (1667-1672)
Pitirim (1672-1673)
Ioakim (1674-1690)
Adrian (1690-1700)
Tikhon (1917-1925)
Sergy (1943-1944)
Alexy (1945-1970)

Synaxes of the Patriarchs
of Moscow and All Russia
Painting by B. I. Muhin

After many years of silence joyous services are again heard in the Cathedral of the Dormition. The jubilee service was conducted at the relics of many Primates of our Church.

The fourteenth Patriarch of Moscow and All Russia Pimen died on May 3, 1990. As the Archimandrite of the Trinity-St. Sergy Lavra he was buried on May 6 in the monastery he loved so much in the Church of All Russian Saints under the Dormition Cathedral.

For nineteen years he headed the largest Orthodox Church in the world. He was a worthy pastor who was always underpinning the Church's authority in an atheist state. Until his death hour he witnessed the swelling in the ranks of the flock and a greater attraction of the Orthodoxy to the nation.

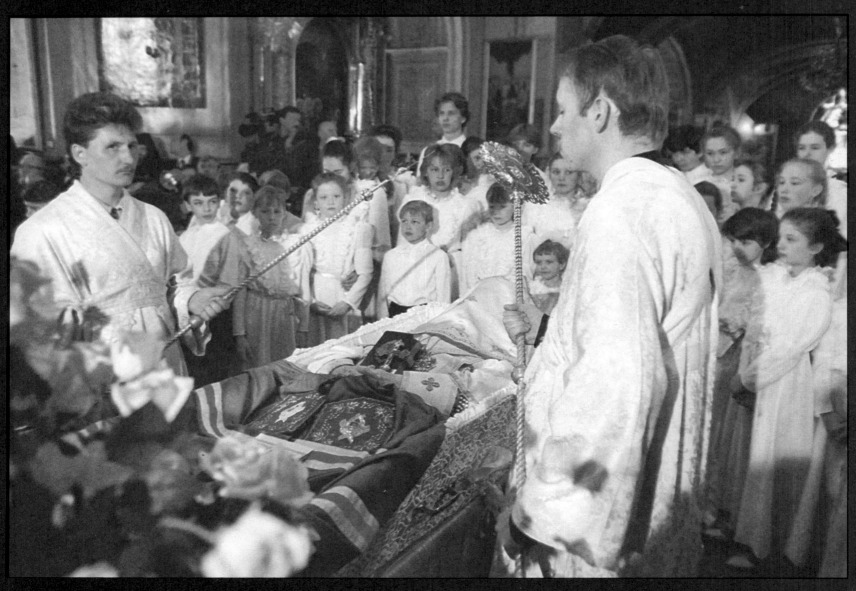

PRAYER

*Let God arise and let His
enemies be scattered,
let them also
that hate Him flee
away from His Countenance.
As the smoke vanisheth,
so may they disappear.
As wax melteth from the fire,
so let demons perish
from the presence of those
that love God,
and place upon themselves
the sign of the Cross
and rejoicingly say:
Hail, O most holy and
life-giving Gross
of the Lord which driveth
away demons by the power
of our Lord Jesus Christ,
Who was crucified upon thee,
descended into the hades,
trampled under His
feet the devil's might
and granted unto us thee,
His precious Cross,
for the driving away
of every enemy.
O most precious and
life-giving Cross!
do help me by the intercession
of the Holy Lady,
Virgin and Theotokos,
and all the saints
unto the ages.
Amen.*

FROM THE AKATHISTOS OF RESURRECTION OF CHRIST

Kontakia 12 and 13

*Singing Thine Most
Glorious Resurrection we laud Thee,
O Jesus Christ, our God!
And we believe that Thou
grant us eternal life. Therefore in this
chosen and Holy Day
let us embrace each other like brothers,
let us forgive because of
Resurrection them who
hate us everything, and let us with one
mouth and one heart cry unto Thee:
Jesus, blessing the ones who bless Thee,
bless the labour I can do; Jesus,
sanctifying those who trust in Thee,
sanctify my wishes
and my intentions.
Jesus, Thee Who promised
to be with the faithful unto the end
of the world, be always with me,
the sinner; Jesus, the Word
of the Hypostasis of the Father,
make my unworthy word
pure to hymn Thee.
Jesus, Pascha saving from death
and leading to life,
settle me within Thy chamber, making
the robe of my soul shine.
Jesus, risen from the dead,
revive our souls. O Jesus Christ,
trampling down Death by death and
bestowing life on those in the tombs,
accept our minor prayer for a savour
of spiritual fragrance and grant
eternal life to us in the tombs
of listlessness, so we hymn Thee:
Alleluia.*

Resurrection of Christ. The most important feast of the Russian Orthodox Church that reveals the most profound mystery of Christ's death and acquiring eternal life, "the joy and peace in Holy Spirit". According to the tradition pascha, eggs and Easter cakes cooked to break the 49-day-long fast, are blessed.

These words joyously resound during the solemn processions accompanied with the inspiring ringing of bells. "Christ is risen!" announces the priest and the people answer three times like one man: "He is risen indeed!"

A faith without works is dead, teaches the Church. Our love of our neighbours demonstrates our sincere goodness and generosity, our love of Jesus Christ.

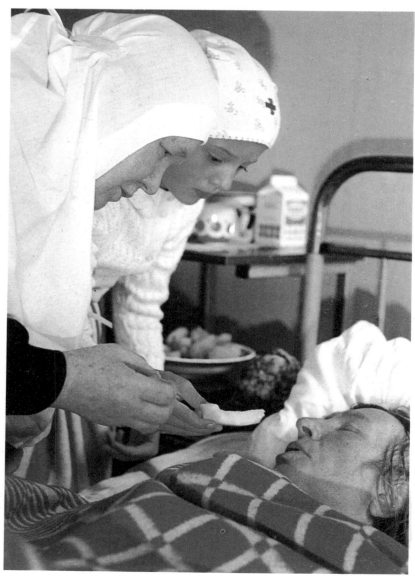

"And though I bestow all my goods to feed the poor, and though I give my body to be burned, and have no charity, it profiteth me nothing. Charity suffereth long, and is kind; charity envieth not; charity vaunteth not itself, is not puffed up, doth not behave itself unseemly, seeketh not her own, is not easily provoked, thinketh no evil; rejoiceth not in iniquity, but rejoiceth in the truth; beareth all things, believeth all things, hopeth all things, endureth all things. Charity never faileth: but whether there be prophecies, they shall fail; whether there be tongues, they shall cease; whether there be knowledge, it shall vanish away".

(1 Cor. 13:3-8)

"And they brought young children to him, that he should touch them: and his disciples rebuked those that brought them. But when Jesus saw it, he was much displeased, and said into them, Suffer the little children to come unto me, and forbid them not: for of such is the kingdom of God. Verily, I say unto you, Whosoever shall not receive the kingdom of God as a little child, he shall not enter therein".

(Mk. 10:13-15)

Aleksy, Archbishop of Zaraisk, Vicar of the Moscow Diocese, head of the Economic Department, attends a lesson of manual labour

"Our Church is, — and this is clearly seen by Us, — embarking on the broad road of social ministry. It is with the feeling of great hope that our society looks upon the Church as the keeper of eternal spiritual and moral values, historical memory and the cultural heritage. To be up to this hope is our historical task. In the time of fateful change the Church in our courtry is far from being an indifferent onlooker. The Church favours the good humanistic aspirations of our society in resolving difficult problems toward building a new life based on law and justice".

(From the Speech of His Holiness Patriarch Aleksy)

"My election by the Sanctified Council of the Russian Orthodox Church as Patriarch of Moscow and All Russia, I accept most thankfully and have nothing against this"—such was the riply of His Eminence Metropolitan Aleksy who was asked to comment on the will of the Local Council expressed by secret ballot.

The ceremonial enthronization of the elect Patriarch took place on June 10, 1990, at the Epiphany Cathedral in Elokhovo, Moscow, in the presence of throngs of Muscovites, participants in and guests of the Local Council of the Russian Orthodox Church.

The senior members of the Holy Synod of the Russian Orthodox Church exclaimed: "Axios." (Worthy), taken up by

the clergy and the laymen. The sacramental moment of the enthronization was done with the words: "The grace divine, which healeth that which is infirm, completeth that which is wanting and guideth providentially the Holy Orthodox Churches, placeth on the throne of Saintly Russian Hierarchs — Petr, Aleksy, Iona, Makary, Filipp, Iov, Ermogen and Tikhon — our Father Aleksy, His Holiness the Patriarch of the Great City of Moscow and All Russia, in the name of the Father, and of the Sun, and of the Holy Spirit. Amen".

After the service His Holiness Patriarch Aleksy II accepted the crozier of St. Petr Metropolitan of Moscow, a great relic of the Russian Orthodox Church, symbolizing the succession of Moscow Primates.

"We ask you to pray ardently for the beneficial success in the primatial work of our father, His Holiness Patriarch Aleksy, and for the abundant grace of Our Lord for his service."

"...Our Church and the people have entered the epoch of great change, marked

by new opportunities and responsibilities. And now, as, perhaps, never before, we have to consider critically our past and our present, to condemn both our inner ills which have been caused by the unfavourable Church existence and what has happened to us through our weakness and imperfection, so that we might 'walk in newness of life'" (Rom. 6. 4).

"... We must spare no effort to foster good qualities in the children, the youth, and the adults who were deprived of religious education, and to confirm them in faithfulness to our Christian tradition."

(From the Message of the Local Council to the Beloved in the Lord Pastors, Honorable Monks and Nuns, and to All the Faithful Children of the Russian Orthodox Church)

„Благодать Господа нашего
Иисуса Христа со всеми вами
Аминь" (Рим 16, 24)

+ Алексий, Патриарх
Московский и всея Руси